THE BIBLICAL ENGINEER

The Holy Temple in Jerusalem

THE BIBLICAL ENGINEER

HOW THE TEMPLE IN JERUSALEM WAS BUILT

MAX SCHWARTZ

ILLUSTRATIONS BY MAX SCHWARTZ

KTAV PUBLISHING HOUSE, INC.
HOBOKEN, N.J. 07030

Copyright© 2002
Max Schwartz
Library of Congress Cataloging-in-Publication Data

Schwartz, Max, 1922–
    The biblical engineer : how the temple in Jerusalem was built / by Max Schwartz.
    p. cm.
Includes bibliographical references and index.
ISBN 0-88125-711-7 — ISBN 0-88125-710-9 (pbk.)
1. Building—Jerusalem—History.   2. Temples—Jerusalem—Design and construction.
3. Temple of Jerusalem (Jerusalem)—History.   4. Jerusalem—Antiquities.   I. Title.
TH16 .S38 2001
690'.63'09569442—dc21

                                                              2001029207

Distributed by
Ktav Publishing House, Inc.
900 Jefferson Street
Hoboken, NJ 07030
201-963-9524 FAX 201-963-0102
Email orders@ktav.com

CONTENTS

Chapter 3—Construction Equipment and Transportation (continued)

Chapter 4—Engineering, Planning, and Logistics   53

Chapter 5—Construction Materials   71

Chapter 6—Building the Temple Mount   82

Chapter 7—Building Antonia Fortress and the Porticos

Chapter 8—The Temple and Courts

Chapter 9—The Siege of Jerusalem

ACKNOWLEDGMENTS

I am greatly indebted to the following friends and colleagues for their advice and their support, and their unstinting help in preparation of this book: Bernie Scharfstein, Publisher, KTAV Publishing House; William J. Peterson, Senior Editor, Fleming H. Revell Company; Dan Bahat of the Israel Ministry of Antiquities; Dr. Ronny Reich of the Rockefeller Museum, Jerusalem; Prof. Arthur Yuwiler and David Wetterberg, fellow members of the California Writers Club; Ilene McGrath, who copyedited the manuscript, and Andrew Gross, who made many valuable suggestions.

Max Schwartz

September 2001
Los Angeles, California

When I attended an international engineering conference in Israel, I thought it was to be a purely professional excursion. I never dreamed it would be the beginning of an unexpected personal quest.

It began on a guided tour through the Old City of Jerusalem. We were in an underground vault adjacent to the Temple Mount. "Overhead you'll see a good example of Herodian workmanship," our guide pointed out. The group moved on, but I paused for a moment.

This is amazing, I thought. A four-part groined vault. It was a very complex structure. The springline, keystones, and vousoirs had to be measured without error so that the four arches met perfectly at the crown. They made this 2000 years ago! I marveled. How did they do it? Even with modern computers and technology, it would take great expertise to carve and fit these stone blocks so accurately.

The rest of the conference sped by, but even after I returned to the United States, I could not shake the fascination with the Temple Mount and the men who built it. On building projects and at work sites around Los Angeles, I continued to imagine myself in King Herod's court designing and building the Temple Mount.

This became an obsession. I decided that the only way to get it off my mind was to go back to Jerusalem for further research. I rented an apartment near the Old City, met with Dan Bahat of the Ministry of Antiquities, and visited the Rockefeller Museum. As I read and studied the Bible and the background of the Temple itself, I began to question my motives. This was not just professional curiosity! I was searching for the history of my people. Backed by my longtime interest in architecture, my working on the Pan American Highway, and my military service with the U.S. Army Corps of Engineers, I felt a strong kinship with those biblical engineers.

I found there were great similarities in the temples of ancient societies, but Israel, with its devotion to one true God, was a notable exception. When the Jews finally settled in the land that God promised them, they wanted a single temple, centrally located where all Israel could worship together. King David found this site, Jerusalem. His son, Solomon, reigning over the economic and military glory years of Israel, built the beautiful Temple on Mount Moriah. The Temple was built of limestone in seven years but stood nearly four centuries until the Babylonian King Nebuchadnezzar destroyed it in 586 BCE.

I learned that centuries later, King Herod, a Jew, hated by his people for being too close with the conquering Romans, tried to prove his devotion to his people by rebuilding the Temple. This second Temple was much larger and more ornate than the first. The faithful came here not only to worship and to sacrifice, but to discuss the Scriptures with learned teachers and rabbis. It was here that talmudic scholar Hillel sat for hours with his disciples in the first century BCE.

As I paced the stones of the Temple Mount, I felt beside me the presence of those master builders who had brought the limestone blocks from the nearby quarry, hauled them on rollers, and hoisted them with giant wooden cranes. I developed a kinship with those master builders. I knew they were using their skills not for the glory of Herod, but for the glory of God.

My interest in ancient engineering has only increased since then. It was more than a professional pilgrimage that took me back to Jerusalem. I thought then that I was in search of the ancient master builders, never suspecting I would discover that their purpose in building so many years ago was to invite people to meet the true Master Builder. After all these centuries, I am living proof that the invitation still stands.

The following excerpts from the *Jewish Encyclopedia* (pp. 85–86) generally describe the construction of Herod's Temple. They were based on *Midrash,* or ancient Jewish commentary on the Scriptures.

In the eighteenth year (20–19 BCE) of his reign, Herod rebuilt the Temple on a more magnificent scale [than the first Temple, built by Solomon]. There are many evidences that he shared the passion for building by which many powerful men of that time were moved. He had adorned many cities and had erected many heathen temples; and it was not fitting that the temple of his capital shall fall beneath these in magnificence. Probably, also, one of his motives was to placate the more pious of his subjects, whose sentiments he had often outraged.

The Jews were loath to have their Temple pulled down, fearing it might not be rebuilt. To demonstrate his good faith, Herod accumulated the materials for the new building before the old one was taken down. The new Temple was rebuilt as rapidly as possible, being finished in a year and a half, although work was in progress on the outbuildings and the courts for eighty years. As it was unlawful for any but the priests to enter the Temple, Herod employed 1,000 of them as masons and carpenters.

The Temple proper as reconstructed by Herod was of the same dimensions as that of Solomon, viz: 60 cubits* long, 20 cubits wide, and 40 cubits high. This space was divided into the Holy of the Holies, and the "Hekal." The former measured 20 by 20 cubits, the latter 20 by 40. At the entrance to the outer Temple hung a veil embroidered in blue, white (byssus), scarlet, and purple. The outer Temple was separated from the Holy of the Holies

*one cubit = 18 inches

by a similar curtain. The outer curtain was folded back on the south side, and the inner one on the north side, so that a priest in entering the Holy of the Holies traversed the outer Temple diagonally. The Holy of the Holies was quite empty. In the Holy Place stood an altar of incense. Near the entrance to the Holy of the Holies, the seven-branched golden candlestick to the south, and the table for showbread to the north. Above the gate to the Temple were golden vines and grape clusters as large as a man. The Temple building had an upper story similar in size to the lower. Side structures as in Solomon's Temple afforded space for three stories of chambers on the north, south, and west sides of the Temple. These chambers were connected by doors; and trapdoors afforded communication from those of one story to those of the story immediately above or below. The whole breadth of the structure including the side buildings was 70 cubits.

East of Herod's Temple, there was, as in Solomon's, a porch 100 cubits wide, 100 cubits high, and 20 cubits deep, thus extending 15 cubits in either side of the Temple. Its gateway, which had no gate, was 20 cubits broad and 70 cubits high. Over the gateway, Herod erected a golden eagle, which was afterward pulled down by the Jews. The front of the porch was covered with gold. It was most brilliant when the rays of the morning sun fell upon it.

The following excerpts from the *Jewish Encyclopedia* (pp. 81–84) generally describe the rituals and personnel of the Temple. They were based on *Midrash,* or ancient Jewish commentary on the Scriptures.

Administration and Service

A board of fifteen appointed officers managed the affairs of the Second Temple. The *Mishnah* records the names of officers and their responsibilities without stating their respective periods of activity. It is presumed they were those appointed in the time of *Agrippa*: (1) Jonathan B. Phinchas, in charge of the seals given in exchange for money to purchase sacrifices; (2) Ahijah, of libations; (3) Mattithiah B. Samuel, of allotments (i.e., the selection of priests for the day); (4) Pethahial, of the nests of fowls (for sacrifices); (5) Ben Ahijah of the health department (treating especially a disease of the bowels caused by bare feet touching the cold marble pavement); (6) Nehunya, of the digging of wells (for the Pilgrims on the highways leading to Jerusalem); (7) Gebini (Gabinimus), of announcements (the Temple crier); (8) Ben Geber, of the gates (opening and closing them); (9) Ben Babi, of the wicks for the candlesticks (*Menorah*); (10) Ben Arza, of the cymbals (leading the music of the *Levites*); (11) Hugras (Hugdas) B. Levi, of the musical instruments; (12) the Garmu family, of the preparation of the showbread; (13) the Abtinas family, of the incense; (14) Eleaiar, of the curtains; and (15) Phinehas, of the vestment.

Temple Treasury

Seven trustees and three cashiers had charge of the Temple treasury. In the courts were thirteen contribution boxes in the shape of ram's horn (*Shofarim*), with narrow necks and broad bases. The half shekel contribution for public sacrifices, etc., was due on the first of the month of *Adar* and was payable by the 25th of the same month. There was a special room called the Secret Chamber, for anonymous donations, out of which fund the worthy poor were supported. Into the Vessel Chamber the people deposited silver and gold vessels. Every thirty days this chamber was opened by the cashiers, who selected such vessels as could be utilized in the Temple, the rest being sold and the proceeds applied to a fund for repairing the Temple building.

Priestly Officials

The priestly officials were the high priest, his deputy, and his two attendants. The guard being composed of three priests and twenty-one *Levites* maintained a strict watch of the Temple. The priests were stationed one at the Chamber of the Flame, one at the Chamber of the Hearth, and one at the Chamber, or *Attic of Abtinas*. The *Levites* kept guard as follows: one at each of the five gates of the mount entrances; one at each of the four corners within the mount enclosure; one at each of the five important gates of the courts; one at each of the four corners within the court; one at the Chamber of Sacrifice; one at the Chamber of Curtains; and one behind the Holy of Holies. The captain of the guards saw that every man was alert, chastising the priest if found asleep at his post, and sometimes even punishing him by burning his shirt upon him as a warning to others.

The priests were divided into twenty-four patrols, which were changed every week. The patrol was quartered partly in the Chamber of the Flame and principally in the Chamber of the Hearth, both of which were on the north side of the inner court. The latter chamber was a capacious one, surmounted by a dome. Half of this chamber extended outside the court to a kind of platform surrounding the courts, which was considered as secular, in contrast to the sacred premises within, where the priests were not allowed to sit down, much less to sleep. A fire was always kept burning in the outer extension, at which the priests might warm their hands and bare feet. Here also they might sit down and rest for a while. At night the elder priests slept here on divans placed on rows of stone steps one above another. The younger priests slept on cushions on the floor, putting their sacred garments under their heads and covering themselves with their secular clothing. The elder priests kept the keys of the temple, putting them at night under a marble slab in the floor; to this slab a ring was attached for lifting it. A priest watched over or slept on the slab until the keys were demanded by the officer in the morning.

The king when visiting the temple had no rights beyond those of the ordinary Israelite: only the kings of the house of David were privileged to sit down in the *Azarah*. The major *Sanhedrin* was composed of 71 members. They sat in the Chamber of Hewn Stone on the extreme north of the priest's hall.

Judiciary

Two tribunals of the minor *Sanhedrin*, each composed of 23 members, sat one by the south gate of the mount and one in front of the hall of the north side. The sessions were held from the morning sacrifice until that of the afternoon. On Sabbaths and Holy Days, to facilitate increased business the major *Sanhedrin* sat outside of the Hel, and the minor *Sanhedrin* assembled in the *Bet Ha-midrash* situated on the mount.

Entrance within the enclosure of the mount was permitted to anyone who was decently attired and who carried no burden. Israelites when ritually unclean and Gentiles were not allowed to pass beyond the *Soreg*, a fence which surrounded the courts at a distance of ten cubits.

Local Divisions

The outer court called the Women's Hall was for the use of ordinary Israelites. The Priest's hall was reserved for the priests and the *Levites*: occasionally, however, men and women presenting sin offerings, sacrifices on which they were required to place the hands, made use of it. At the festivals, to accommodate the large crowds, all Israelites were permitted to enter the Priest's hall, on which occasion the curtain of the vestibule was raised to show the people the interior of the *Hekal*. The people, though tightly packed, were able to find sufficient space in which to prostrate themselves, this being one of the miracles associated with the Temple. The people crowded to within 11 cubits behind the Holy of Holies.

Water Supply

Another phenomenon was the water supply. A spring rising below the Holy of the Holies from an opening as narrow as the antennae of a locust increased, when it reached the entrance to the

Hekal, to the side of a wart-thread; at the entrance to the vestibule it assumed the size of a wool-thread; and at the house of David it became an overflowing brook. This spring is referred to in the [passage "and behold waters issued out from under the threshold of the house . . . at the south side of the altar"]; it was the mysterious spring that filled the bath of Ishmael the high priest, situated by the Attic of Abtinas on the south of the court, at the water-gate. There was another bath, in a passage under the Chamber of the Hearth, for the use of any ordinary priest who might become ritually unclean. This was reached by a winding staircase. The priest, having bathed, dried himself by the fire; he then dressed and returned to his comrades above, with whom he waited until the gates were opened when he left the *azarah*, being unfit for service till sunset of the same day.

Order of Service

The order of the priests' daily service in the Temple was as follows: One of the priests arose early and bathed before the arrival of the officers, who usually came about cockcrow. The officers knocked at the door of the Chamber of Hearth and the priest opened it. He called to the priest who had bathed, and ordered him to decide by lot which of the priests should serve that day. The officer then took the keys and entered through the wicket (*pishpush*) of the door to the *azarah*, followed by the priests who formed the patrol, each holding two torches. The patrol was divided into two sections, one going through the colonnade on the east, and one on the west, the section meeting on the south side at the chamber where they prepared the baked cake for the meal offering. The priests now asked one another "Is all well?" and received the answer "All is well." The officer assigned by lot the making of the bread. Similarly he selected the priest to clean the altar of ashes, his comrades uttering the warning: "Be careful not to touch the sacred vessels before thou sanctifiest [by washing] the hands and feet at laver; and see that the coal shovel is in its place near the inclined plank or bridge leading to the altar." Proceeding without any light save that of the pyre on the altar, he disappeared below, and was next heard operating the machinery for raising the laver from the well. This consisted of a wooden wheel and shaft and a chain, a device designed by the high priest. The noise caused by this operation fixed the time of the washing of hands and feet. The priests took the silver *mahtah* and ascended the altar; pushing the large coal aside, he took a shovel full of ashes and charred wood and, descending, turned north-ward and deposited the ashes in a heap on the floor three hand-breadths from the *kebesh*, where also the ashes from the golden altar and the candlestick were placed.

The Sacrifice

The officers then ordered the priests to decide by lot who should slaughter the sacrificial lamb, who should sprinkle the blood, who should clean the ashes from the golden altar and from the golden candlestick, and who should attend the sacrifices in de-tail. This being done, the officer commanded: "Go ye and see if it is time to commence the sacrificial services." Mounting to an em-inence of the Temple, they looked toward the east, until at length one shouted, "The light has appeared."

The Abattoir

The slaughter of the lamb was effected as follows: The front legs were bound to the hind legs, the head pointing south with its face toward the west. The *shohet* stood facing the west. The morning *tamid* was slaughtered at the northwest corner, that of the afternoon at the northeast corner, of the altar at the second ring. There were twenty-four rings in four rows, fixed to the floor on hinges; in these the heads of the animals were held in posi-tion. The priest who received the blood in a basin stood facing the south. He sprinkled blood on both sides of the northeast and southwest corners of the altar. The removal of the hide and the dissection of the carcass were shared by the priests and were fol-lowed by the meal offering. This accomplished, the priests went to the Chamber of Hewn Stone. There the officer directed them to recite one benediction and to read the Ten Commandments and the *Shema,* after which they blessed the people. On the Sab-baths, they blessed also with "love, brotherhood, peace, and friendship" the patrol that was about to go off duty.

Finally, the priests drew lots for the incense service, and the var-ious assignments were made, only those who had not been previ-ously selected being admitted to the ballot. The priests who were not to share in the service of the day now removed their priestly garments and then, having delivered them to an attendant who placed them in their proper lockers, dressed themselves in their secular clothes and retired from the *azarah* till their next turn.

The Biblical Engineer

Throughout history, people have had a passion to expand their knowledge of biblical times. Their search has inspired countless studies and books. Today thousands of tourists visiting the Temple Mount in Jerusalem wonder, "How did they plan and build these structures? What methods were used to transport and place such large stone blocks? How did they measure and shape these blocks to fit so perfectly into masonry arches? What tools and technical knowledge were available to these artisans?" Some have inquired, "Who were the biblical Master Builders? What kind of people were the masons, carpenters, and smiths that King Herod ordered to build the Temple Mount?"

Answers to some of these questions may be found in the Bible; in the writings of Flavius Josephus, a Jewish historian of the first century CE; and in the Mishnah, a collection of Jewish oral laws compiled in the second century CE. Other answers are continually being uncovered through archaeological study of the remains of buildings, tools, weapons, and ships.

The modern-day architect, surveyor, and military and civil engineer, who have much in common with their biblical counterparts, can apply the laws of physics to prove that the ancient construction methods described here were both realistic and practical. This book portrays how biblical builders may have designed and constructed the Temple Mount. It depicts the master builders from the Hellenistic Period (332–37 BCE) to the time of the Roman destruction of the Second Temple (70 CE).

Some of the Temple builders were descendants of exiles who returned from captivity in Babylon and brought back to the Holy Land many skills absorbed from the advanced Babylonian and

Figure 1-1
Blacksmiths working at an ancient kiln

Figure 1-2A
Section through a stone kiln

Figure 1-2B
Section through a stone kiln

Figure 1-3
Pumping a leather bellow

Persian cultures. The Babylonians and Persians inherited much of their technical knowledge from the earlier Mesopotamian cultures, such as the Sumerians. The Sumerians, who were skilled in many areas, developed bricks of great strength and durability. They mixed wet clay with chopped reeds and fired the bricks in kilns, using fuels from asphalt that seeped to the ground surface. They also extracted metals from ore. Figure 1-1 shows these early smiths at work.

Figures 1-2A and 1-2B illustrate how stone kilns were constructed. The bellows blew oxygen-bearing air into the fire to raise the temperature in the kiln. A typical leather bellow is shown in Figure 1-3.

The Biblical Period, defined here as 1200 BCE to 100 CE, was a time of great inventions, such as Rhodes' computer.[1] Simple surveying instruments were developed during that time to lay out construction projects accurately.

During the Exilic Period (sixth century BCE), many changes occurred along the eastern shores of the Mediterranean Sea. Seafaring Phoenicians often called on ports of the Holy Land, introducing the skills of shipbuilding, carpentry, and rigging. Ship's rigging included the ropes and other equipment that support the sails and lift heavy cargo. Also Greek merchants and artisans who settled in the port towns brought their own scientific and mathematical traditions, which would merge with those of Egypt, Mesopotamia, and other areas of the Ancient Near East.

Evidence of human settlement on the site where Jerusalem now stands goes back 5,000 years. City walls were first built there in the eighteenth century BCE. The earliest known documents mentioning Jerusalem by name date to approximately 1400 BCE. When the city was captured by David in 1000 BCE., it was a Jebusite city, but the Jebusites were ultimately absorbed into the Israelite population.

In 586 BCE, the Holy City was conquered and destroyed—along with Solomon's Temple—by Nebuchadnezzar II of Babylon. About fifty years later, Cyrus the Great of Persia defeated the

[1] The Rhodes Calculator, also known as the Antikythera Mechanism, is the most sophisticated scientific instrument surviving from antiquity. It is an astronomical calculator with precision gearing and is accurate to 1:40,000. The device was built in Rhodes in about 80 BCE and was discovered in 1900 in a sunken shipwreck off the island of Antikythera, near Crete. Study of its mechanism enabled historians of science to reassess the high technology of ancient Greece.

Babylonians and permitted the Jews to return and rebuild the city and Temple.

Jews returning to Jerusalem from exile joined with the local inhabitants to restore the damaged city and Solomon's Temple. Master builders, civil engineers, city planners, and craftsmen of all types reconstructed the Temple and inner courts, expanded the city walls, and repaved the streets. They also built houses for those drawn from the countryside to work in Jerusalem.

In 332 BCE, Alexander the Great added Jerusalem to his empire, and when he died in 323 BCE, his empire was split up among his lieutenants. For the next 150 years, two of these smaller empires, the Ptolemaic Empire in Egypt and the Seleucid Empire in Syria, struggled for suprememacy over Judea. The Ptolemies held the upper hand at first, establishing control of Judea in 301 BCE. In 198 BCE, however, the Seleucid king, Antiochus III, managed to wrest control of Judea and Jerusalem away from his Ptolemaic rival. The Seleucids maintained control over Jerusalem until the outbreak of the Maccabean Revolt in 164 BCE, when the Hasmoneans took over and ruled the city. Figure 1-4 shows the Hasmonean *Family Tree* descending from Mattathias and Simon. Jerusalem remained under Hasmonean rule until the city fell into Roman hands in 63 BCE, when Antipater, an Idumean and father of Herod the Great, was established as procurator.

Figure 1-4
The Hasmonean family tree

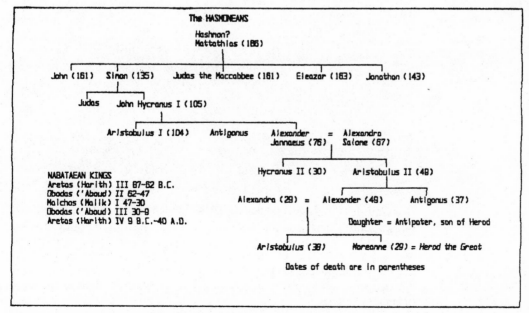

The chronology of Jerusalem's rulers can be summarized as follows:

BCE

1400	Abdi-Heba, an Egyptian vassal, is Jerusalem's local chieftain, corresponding with the Pharaoh Akhenaten.
1000	David captures the Jebusite city.
586	Nebuchadnezzer II of Babylon captures and destroys the city.
539	Cyrus the Great of Persia defeats the Babylonians and permits the Jews to rebuild the city and Temple.
332	Alexander the Great adds Jerusalem to his empire.
323	Alexander dies.
301	Ptolemy I establishes Ptolemaic control of Jerusalem.
198	Antiochus III, the Seleucid king, wrests control of Jerusalem from the Ptolemies.
164	Maccabean Revolt ends Seleucid control of Jerusalem.
63	Pompey brings the city under Roman control.

The population of the Holy Land exploded during the Hasmonean and Herodian Periods. The Judean towns that sprang up were inhabited by craftsmen, merchants, laborers, and priests. In 20 BCE Herod the Great was able to conscript a work force of over 10,000 from this diversified population to greatly expand the Temple Mount. An ossuary was found inscribed with the Hebrew words "Simon the Temple Builder," attesting that Jews were involved in building construction. King Herod recruited hundreds of local skilled stonecutters and imported experienced Greek quarrymen.

During this time, the Holy Land was multilingual. Common people spoke only Aramaic and Hebrew, while those involved in trade and construction also spoke Greek. Priests and the ruling class were conversant in Aramaic, Hebrew, Greek, and Latin. Stone signs addressed to the Hebrews were cut in Aramaic and those to the Gentiles, or non-Jews, were in Greek and Latin. Jewish masons identified stone blocks with Hebrew letters. Technicians and engineers used the Greek symbols, numerals, and formulas, which were more precise than the Hebrew. Since the Bible makes almost no reference to mathematical science, we cannot be sure of the state of its development in biblical Israel. Some have argued that it was relatively unsophisticated and point to 1 Kings 7:23, which describes a vessel in Solomon's Temple and gives the ratio of its circumference to its diameter as 3.

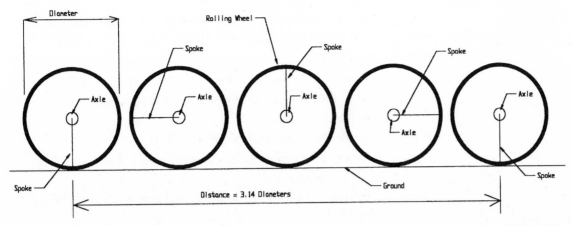

Figure 1-5
How the value of pi was determined
from a wheel

We know today, as the Ancient Greeks knew then, that this ratio is closer to 3.14, which the Greeks designated as the constant pi. Figure 1-5 shows how the value of pi was found graphically by measuring the track made by a wheel on the ground. The distance traveled by the wheel in one rotation was 3.14 times the diameter of the wheel.

Geometry and trigonometry were used long before Herod began to expand the Temple Mount. Many of the great Greek mathematicians had recorded their principles on rolls of papyrus paper. Herod's engineers had access to the scientific writings of Thales of Miletus (c 640–546 BCE), Pythagorus (c 580–500 BCE), Euclid (c 300 BCE), Archimedes (c 287–212 BCE), Hipparchus (c 160–125 BCE), and Ptolemy (c 100–170 CE).

A *Time Line* of important events that occurred from 170 BCE to 70 CE is shown below:

BCE

170	Antiochus IV Epiphanes pillages the Jerusalem Temple treasury while returning from a campaign in Egypt.
167	Antiochus permits the Hellenizers' pagan worship at the Temple.
166	Mattathias the Hasmonean dies.
164	Judah Maccabee leads a revolt against the Seleucids, occupies Jerusalem, consecrates and rededicates the Temple.
161	Judah Maccabee dies.
152	Jonathan the Hasmonean, Judah's younger brother, becomes high priest. Hasmonean Period begins.
143	Jonathan dies and is succeeded by his brother Simon.

139	Roman senate recognizes independence of Judea.
134	Simon dies and is succeeded by John Hyrcanus I.
104	John Hyrcanus I dies and is succeeded by Aristobulus I, who is the first Hasmonean to adopt the title of king.
103	Aristobulus I dies and is succeeded by Alexander Jannaeus.
87	Antikythera mechanism is invented.
76	Alexander Jannaeus dies and his wife Salone Alexandra reigns as regent.
67	Salome Alexandra dies and her son Hyrcanus II succeeds her.
63	In the midst of a power struggle between Hyrcanus II and his brother Aristobulus II, the Roman general Pompey enters Judea and Jerusalem and annexes it to Rome. Hellenistic Period ends.
54	Crassus plunders the Temple.
51	Ptolemy XIII rules Egypt with his sister, Cleopatra.
49	Aristobulus II is murdered.
48	Antipater becomes first procurator of Judea.
46	Antipater appoints his sons Phaesael and Herod to be the governors of Jerusalem and Galilee, respectively.
44	Julius Caesar is assassinated.
43	Antipater is assassinated.
39	Herod is made king of Judea by the Roman senate. Judea booms in culture and prosperity.
37	Roman Herodian Period begins. Hasmonean Period ends.
35	Herod marries Mareanne, granddaughter of Aristobulus II, and appoints her brother Aristobulus III high priest.
34	Herod begins restoring and expanding the Temple Mount.
31	Vitruvius of Rome writes *Ten Books on Architecture.*
30	Cleopatra, queen of Egypt, commits suicide.
30	Hyrcanus II dies.
27	Augustus becomes first Roman emperor.
8–4	Jesus of Nazareth is born.
4	Herod the Great dies. Kingdom is divided among Herod's sons: Archelaus (Judea), Herod Antipas (Galilee and Peraea), and Philip (northern region).

CE

| 6 | Zealots begin resistance. Archelaus is deposed, and Judea becomes a Roman protectorial province. |

6–9	Coponius serves as Roman procurator in Judea.
14	Emperor Tiberius (d. 37) begins his reign.
21	The Roman geographer Pliny is born.
34	Philip dies. Northern third of Judea is added to Roman province of Syria.
37	Agrippa, Philip's nephew, rules. Flavius Josephus (Joseph ben Matthias) is born.
39	Herod Antipas is deposed.
40	Caligula attempts to have a statue of himself installed in the Jerusalem Temple.
41	Local rule in Judea is restored by Emperor Claudius I, who places Agrippa I, Herod's grandson, on the throne.
44	King Agrippa I dies, and Claudius returns Judea to procutorial rule.
50	Agrippa II reigns.
54	Emperor Nero reigns.
57	Josephus joins the Pharisees.
62	Procurator Albinus rules.
63	Work continues on the Temple Mount.
64	Procurator Gessius Florus rules.
66	Jewish War with Rome begins.
69	Vespasian is declared emperor of Rome.
70	Jerusalem is sieged and destroyed by Titus.

Herod the Great's predecessors and descendants are listed below:

- Antipater I (grandfather)
- Antipater II (father)
- Herod the Great
- Archelaus (son, deposed 6 CE)
- Herod Antipas (son, died 39 CE)
- Philip (son, died 44 CE)
- Herod Agrippa I (nephew of Philip, died 44 CE)
- Aristobulus (son)
- Agrippa II (son of Agrippa I, reigned 50 CE)

The following chapters first describe the geographic environment and natural resources of the Holy Land. Then the state of science and construction methods used by the Temple Mount builders are illustrated. Finally, this book closes with the building and destruction of the Temple Mount.

CHAPTER 2

The Land and Its Natural Resources

Land of Milk and Honey

The Holy Land was more than just "a Land of Milk and Honey." It was rich in fertile soil, valuable minerals, black asphalt, limestone mountains, and hot deserts. It also benefited both culturally and economically from a high level of trade as it sat at the crossroads of land and sea routes between Europe, Asia, and Africa.

Through the ages the land's name and inhabitants changed. In Abraham's time, the land was known as *Canaan,* which probably meant "Sunken" or "Low Lands." Then, during the reigns of King David and King Solomon, it became *Eretz Yisrael,* or the Land of Israel. After Solomon's death, his kingdom split into *Israel* (north) and *Judah* (south). By the Hellenistic Period, the area around Jerusalem would become known as *Judea,* and after a series of revolts during the period of Roman domination, the Romans would rename it *Palestina,* which was the name of the southern coastal region.

Throughout the centuries, different societies controlled the region for varying periods: Egyptians, Phoenicians, Israelites, Assyrians, Babylonians, Persians, Greeks, Romans, Arabs, Ottoman Turks, and most recently Israelis. Each left its imprint on the land. Successive societies modified buildings or constructed new houses, fortifications, waterworks, and roads, but using the existing foundations and stone blocks where they could. Many structures found in archacological sites were composites of different periods and cultures.

Although the Holy Land was small, it was unique in its diverse topographic and climatic conditions. Figure 2-1 shows the Mediterranean Sea, Judean hills, Negev deserts, Lake Galilee, and the Dead Sea. This land is only 150 miles long and 54 miles at its widest. The region encompasses about 6,000 square miles of arid

deserts, green farmlands, and lofty mountains. Its location amid the surrounding areas can be seen in Figure 2-2. Situated on the Mediterranean Sea's eastern shore, it had many popular ports-of-call for ships trading between Europe and Africa.

Figure 2-3 illustrates its five major geographic regions:

- *Galil,* or Galilee, is a mountainous area with peaks over 3,000 feet above sea level.
- *Valleys* include the Zebulun Valley southeast of Haifa, the Valley of Jezreel, the Jordan Valley, and the Bet-Shean Valleys.
- *Coastal Plain* extends from Haifa to Migdal Gad.
- *Hill Areas* are Shomron (Samaria), the Hills of Ephraim, and the Judean Hills, including Jerusalem.
- *Negev* is a triangular area between Elath and the extreme south.

Unlike many larger countries, this small land boasted two inland seas: *Sea of Galilee* and the *Dead Sea.* The Sea of Galilee, which is actually a lake, is about 700 feet below sea level and fed by the Jordan River. The Dead Sea is a body of water in a deep canyon 1,300 feet below sea level. It is the lowest spot on the face

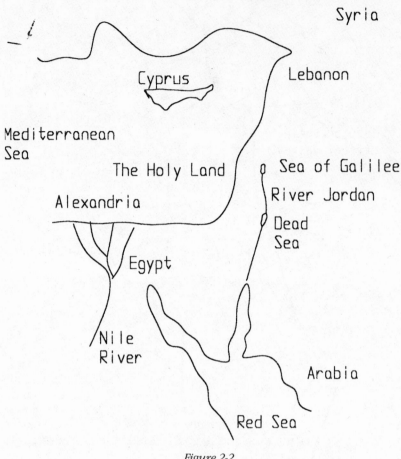

Figure 2-2
The Holy Land and surrounding area

of the earth. In the ancient past, this body of water was called the Sea of Salt *(Yam Ha-Melach)*. In 384–322 BCE, Aristotle and Strado called this inland sea *Lake of Asphalt*. Early pilgrims referred to it as *Devil's Sea,* and the Greeks named it the *Dead Sea.* Figure 2-4, a profile along the Jordan River, shows Lake Galilee, the Dead Sea, and nearby mountain ranges.

Figures 2-5 and 2-6, depicting sections through the Holy Land, show its extreme geographic changes. The land rises from sea level at the Mediterranean shore to 2,500-foot elevation at Jerusalem, then descends rapidly to 1,300 feet below sea level at the Dead Sea. This land rests on deep strata of chalk and limestone. Sediment filled the great chasm in the surface of the earth.

When Jerusalem was conquered by David, it covered only about 12 acres on a V-shaped mountain ridge, as shown on Figure 2-7. The town measured about 1,250 feet north to south and 400 feet east to west. Thick walls and sheer cliffs protected it-

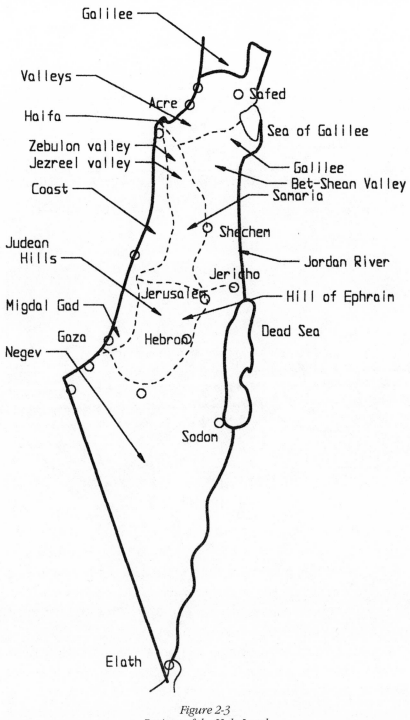

Figure 2-3
Regions of the Holy Land

crowded houses and narrow, crooked streets. This little community was surrounded on three sides by steep slopes that were
easily defendable. Most important, a natural spring, called *Gihon,* was nearby.

This mountain ridge between the Mediterranean and the

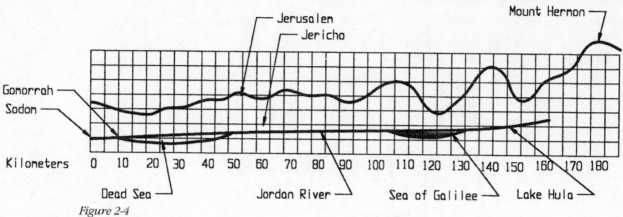

Figure 2-4
Profile along the Jordan River

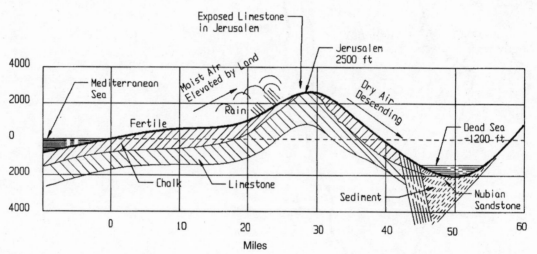

Figure 2-5
Section through the Holy Land

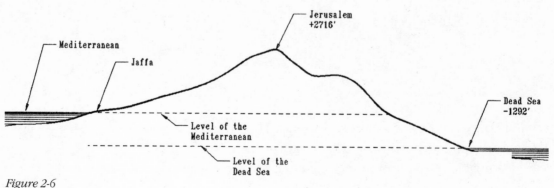

Figure 2-6
A topographic profile through the
Holy Land

desert range also formed a climatic border between the fertile west and the dry eastern desert. Figure 2-8 is a topographic map of Jerusalem and its surrounding area. The contour lines indicate elevations in 10-meter intervals.

Jerusalem was near the crossing of ancient caravan routes. The north-south paths went along the Judean Mountains and the east-west routes linked the Mediterranean Sea to the Jordan Valley. The major towns in Israel are shown in Figure 2-9.

The major sub-regions of the Second Temple period (see Figure 2-10) include Galilee, Samaria, Tabiah, Judea, and Idumaea. This map also shows the ancient towns.

King David built the City of David above the Kidron Valley southeast of Jerusalem. Figure 2-11 shows the walls and towers around this ancient city, which was near the present town of Silwan. Some believed this town to be the resting place of King David. Today houses and caves in Silwan cluster on both sides of the valley.

Figure 2-12 shows the topography and walls of Jerusalem at the time of King Herod. Its water source is referred to in the Bible as the *Pool of Shelah* (Neh. 3:15) and as *Pool of Siloam* (John 9:7). The reservoir of Hezekiah was identified with the *Pool of Shiloam* (2 Kings 20:20; 2 Chron. 32:30). This spring was the main source of an underground water tunnel constructed by Hezekiah in 701 BCE to ensure a constant supply of spring water to the city of Jerusalem.

Silwan is a living example of the housing in biblical times. Figure 2-13 shows a typical house interior of that time. Many of the houses are built of stone blocks, with recent additions made of modern concrete blocks. The roofs are flat and plastered to collect water from the occasional rains. Roof curbs prevent the rainwater from running off except where a pipe carries water to a barrel or to an underground cistern.

Silwan's stone houses, constructed on the steep slopes of the Kidron Valley, are random clusters of blocks, each attached to an existing structure. People, as well as donkeys and goats, use dirt paths connecting the houses. A narrow paved road winds at the bottom of the Valley to the Gihon Spring and Siloam Pool. The south wall of the Temple Mount looms above the village.

Climate

The Holy Land has extreme differences in weather. The climate of the coastal plain is mild and subtropical because of the two

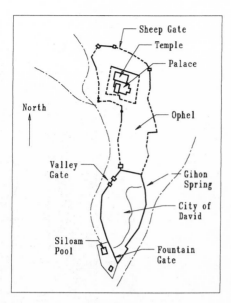

Figure 2-7
City of David
In King David's time
Jerusalem was confined
to a hill known as the
City of David (Dan Bahat,
Carta's Historical Atlas
of Jerusalem)

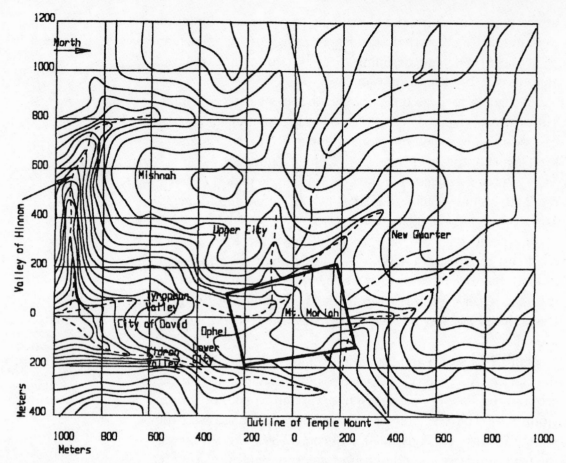

Figure 2-8
Topography around Jerusalem
Note: Contour lines at
10-meter intervals

mountain ranges running parallel to the coastline. These mountains cause moist air to collect along the western areas while dry hot air settles in the Jordan Valley.

Prevailing winds in the eastern Mediterranean divide the country into three natural climatic zones. The northern zone has an abundance of rainwater, the central zone has moderate moisture, and the southern zone lacks rainfall. Because of the unique weather cycles in the Holy Land, crops grow best in the winter. The dead season is during summer, when dry air and intense heat desiccate the vegetation. Intermittent rains usually start in mid-October, peak in January, and end in March.

Natural Resources

Minerals

Valuable minerals are found in many parts of the Holy Land. Copper for tools, manganese for steel, and barite for paints are mined near Elath. The Dead Sea produces iodine and bromine

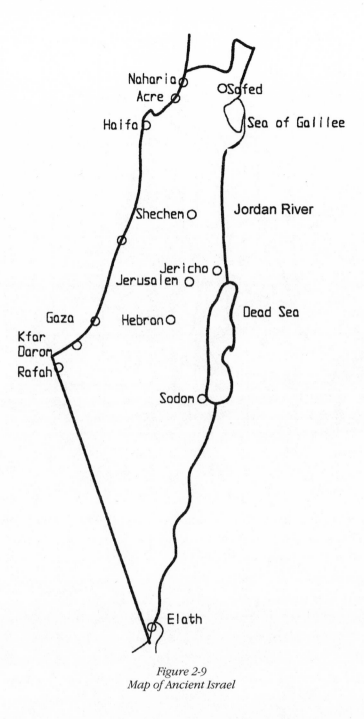

Figure 2-9
Map of Ancient Israel

for medicine, calcium for ceramics, and sodium chloride for preservatives. Glass sands are extracted at Beersheva, while clay and basalt for building material are found near the Lebanon border. Pozzuolana, a natural cement, is quarried near the Sea of Galilee. Bituminous limestone is excavated near Haifa and Jerusalem, and marble is quarried near Gezer. Other mineral resources include sulfur for textiles, gypsum for plaster, fire clay, kaolin, and feldspar for ceramics.

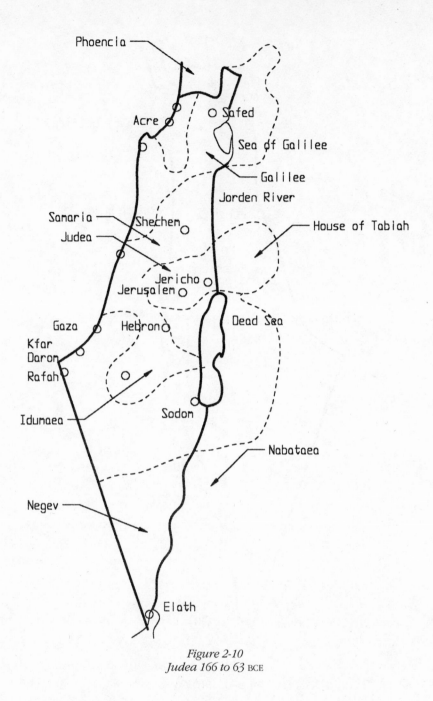

Figure 2-10
Judea 166 to 63 BCE

Although the Dead Sea has no fish, it is rich in minerals. Its water is ten times saltier than seawater. Cleopatra used its salts to beautify herself.

The most important geological characteristic of Jerusalem is the massive limestone outcrop upon which the city was built. Limestone is easy to cut and use as a building material. Because it has a high content of calcium carbonate, it is also a raw material for the manufacture of cement and lime.

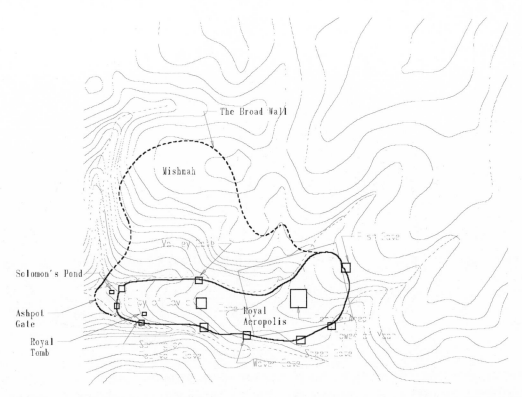

Figure 2-11
Topography around City of David

Timber

Trees in the Holy Land grow slowly because of the limited rainfall. Although the forests contained pines, oaks, and terebinths, the people have always been reluctant to cut the trees for construction. Therefore, they used stone whenever possible and imported lumber.

During biblical times great quantities of timber were available from the forests of Lebanon and Macedonia. Cut timber was transported by ships and rafts and then carried overland by cart to Jerusalem and other major towns.

Cedars of Lebanon are evergreen trees similar to pine trees. When young, these trees are pyramidal in shape, and when old, they develop massive trunks and large table-like branches. Cedar wood was used for ships and buildings throughout the ancient Middle East.

Metals

The ancient civilizations could not have flourished without metal weapons and tools. The importance of the blacksmith was even reflected in ancient mythology. In Canaanite mythology, the Ugaritic deity Kothar-wa-Hasis is depicted as both a producer of weapons and a skilled metal craftsman, and in Greek and Roman

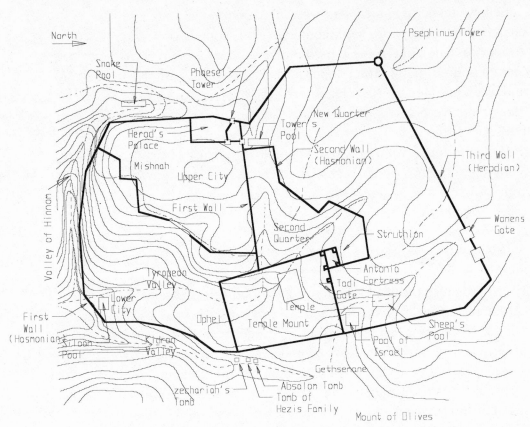

Figure 2-12
Plan of the Old City of Jerusalem

> *The bill was a rocky ascent that declined by degrees toward the east parts of the city, till it came to an elevated level. This hill it was which Solomon, who was the first of our kings, by divine revelation, encompassed with a wall; it was of excellent workmanship upwards, and round the top of it. He also built a wall below, beginning at the bottom, which was encompassed by a deep valley; and at the south side he laid rocks together and bound them one to another with lead, and included some of the inner parts, till it proceeded to a great height, and till both the largeness of the square edifice and its altitude were immense, and till the vastness of the stones in the front were plainly visible on the outside. . . . (Josephus, Ant Book VI Chapter XI)*

mythology, the Roman god Vulcan was said to have been a blacksmith.

Ancient craftsmen found many types of metal-bearing ores in and around the Holy Land. From these ores, they refined iron and copper, which they cast and hammered into ornaments, tools, and weapons.

Copper mining and smelting began at Timna, near Elath, during the Chalcolithic Period (fifth millennium BCE). Wandering hunters heated green malachite stones to form nodules of copper metal. They gathered, smelted, and poured the nodules into clay forms. Later, better kilns were developed which could extract 85 percent of the copper metal from the ore.

Bellows made of animal skin were used to force air into the charcoal fire below iron pots containing the copper ore. The copper became fluid in these high-temperature stone furnaces. Smiths poured the molten copper into clay molds to cast tools and weapons. Metalworkers hammered the copper into utensils and protective helmets and clothing. Copper ingots were also traded for other goods.

Figure 2-13
Interior of a typical stone house

Midianites mined and processed copper at the time of Moses. Many copper mines were worked between the Dead Sea and the Gulf of Aqaba as early as 2500 BCE. One deposit at Timna, now called *Solomon's Mines,* may have supplied King Solomon with copper.

Although copper tools could be sharpened, they were not as durable as stone implements. Also they were not tough enough. The smiths discovered that when they added tin to copper, a harder metal, bronze, was formed. Bronze was workable and suitable for weapons and tools, such as daggers, swords, lances, javelins, and spears. Smiths also manufactured bronze protective articles and clothing such as shields, helmets, breastplates, and leg guards. Bronze tools were important because of their strength and resistance to corrosion even in salt water. A further advance in metallurgy occurred when smiths added zinc to the copper-tin alloy to produce brass.

Although iron was well known, it was rare in the Holy Land. It was once thought that the Hittites and later the Philistines kept the process of smelting iron secret and thereby maintained a monopoly on iron-making, although scholars no longer take such notions seriously. The Bible, nonetheless, does record the fact that the Philistines did not allow the Israelites to own forges, thereby forcing them to buy all of their tools from the Philistines:

> Now there was no smith found throughout all the land of Israel; for the Philistines said: "Lest the Hebrews make them swords or spears"; but all the Israelites went down to the Philistines, to sharpen every man his plowshare, and his coulter, and his axe, and his mattock. And the price of the filing was a pim for the mattocks, and for the coulters, and for the forks with three teeth, and for the axes; and to set the goods. (1 Sam 13:19–21)

During King David's reign, the Philistine monopoly on smelting, forging, and smithing iron was finally broken. Israelites were able to make their own arrowheads, swords, and tools, and these were superior to the bronze ones used before. Iron swords and daggers were sharper and more durable than the bronze blades.

Israelite craftsmen smelted and forged iron points for their plows, shovels, and other earth-working tools. Working in small workshops and bazaars in Jerusalem, they also fashioned weapons, tools, musical instruments, and household utensils.

Traveling blacksmiths, carrying hammers, bellows, tongs, and anvils, were popular not only for their skill in making and repairing metal but also as a source of information about other communities.

Ancient smiths made iron objects in two stages. First, they extracted the iron metal from iron ore through smelting, which consisted of heating the ore beyond the melting point of iron. Smelting was done in the presence of an oxidizing agent, usually charcoal. Lumps of iron mixed with slag and charcoal were called *blooms.*

In the second phase, the *smithing,* the bloom is worked by a smith. He needs only a bellows and a *tuyere,* which is a conical clay object that holds the tip of the bellows and forces the blast of air into the burning charcoal. When the bloom is heated to 1200 degrees F, the pure iron separates from the slag, the inert part of the ore. The smith then pours the molten iron into clay forms to produce weapons, tools, or other iron objects. He hardens some of the items by heating and quenching them in water or oil.

Summary

At the time of the Bible, the Holy Land was rich in natural resources. The people were self-sufficient in most of the raw materials that an advanced society required. Only timber, zinc, and tin were imported.

Because the geography of the land varied from lofty mountains to the lowest valleys of the world, its climate and topography were unique. It was truly the *Promised Land.*

CHAPTER 3

Construction Equipment and Transportation

PART 1 CONSTRUCTION EQUIPMENT

Architecture and engineering activity in the Holy Land was at its height during the first century BCE. It was the time of Hasmonean and Herodian palaces, fortresses, temples, and tombs. This was also the period of major city planning and construction of waterworks, sewerage, and highways.

Hasmonean Royalty

Hasmonean rule began in 152 BCE, when Jonathan became high priest, although it was only with Aristobulus I in 104 BCE that the Hasmoneans began to use the title "king." After only one year on the throne, Aristobulus was succeeded by his son, John Hyrcanus. When John Hyrcanus died in 76 BCE, his two sons, Hyrcanus II and Aristobulus II, were too young to rule, and therefore his widow, Alexandra, became queen. The end of the Hasmonean dynasty came soon after her death in 67 BCE. As the two sons were struggling for the right of succession, the Roman general Pompey was able to turn Judea into a Roman tributary. Hyrcanus II was reduced to the role of "ethnarch," while the real power was wielded by Antipater, an Idumean Jew and the father of *Herod the Great,* who held the position of "procurator" (administrator). The Holy Land would soon become another province of the Roman Empire, like Gaul, Egypt, and Greece.

At the time of Hasmonean rule, Jewish stonemasons built the *Tomb of Zachariah* and the *Tomb of Absalom* in the Kidron Valley. They cut the monuments out of a solid rock outcrop as shown on Figures 3-1 and 3-2. Zachariah's tomb had an Egyptian-style pyramidal roof, supported by Ionic pilasters chiseled from stone walls. The Tomb of Absalom had a circular conical roof that

Figure 3-1
Tomb of Zachariah

rested on a square platform decorated with a wreathed frieze. Both tombs reflect Greek and Egyptian styles.

Herod's Engineers

After a failed attempt in 40 BCE to restore Hasmonean rule in Judea, the Roman Senate made Herod the Great the king of Judea. From the perspective of architecture and engineering, one of most important royal decrees was his decision in 20 BCE to expand and rebuild the Temple Mount. He selected the best engineers and architects to plan this project. They chose the necessary equipment and went abroad to observe foreign techniques.

Many important engineering and architectural treatises from this era still exist today, and therefore we know a great deal about the tools and techniques available to Herod's architects and engineers. One of the most important of these treatises was Vitruvius's *Ten Books of Architecture.* Marcus Vitruvius Pollio, a Roman architect/engineer, who wrote his treatises between 46 and 30 BCE, was commissioned by Julius Caesar and later Emperor Augustus as imperial architect/engineer. In his writing, Vitruvius quoted Herodotus, Aristotle, Theophrastus, and other great thinkers that preceded him. He described the proper use of masonry, wood, and metals.

Herod's engineers and architects were likely familiar with the writings of Archimedes, Plutarch, Livy, and Polybius regarding mathematics, machines, cranes, and pulleys. They may also have drawn on the rich resources of Egypt, which had been an important architectural center for centuries. In addition to her important architectural achievements such as the pyramids, there was also the city of Alexandria, with its great library, a vital center of learning. The Great Pyramid of Giza, which was 20 stories high and covered 15 acres, had been built centuries before the Jerusalem Temple, and therefore the technical knowledge and experience required for acquiring the gigantic building materials and organizing the massive labor forces were not new. Thousands of workers were conscripted to cut and place the stone blocks of the Temple. The workmen cut the blocks at a nearby quarry, hauled them on wood sleds over ramps, and levered them into place.

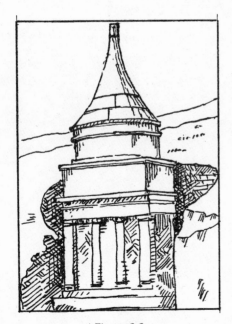

Figure 3-2
Tomb of Absalom

Hand Tools

Herod's craftsmen used stone and metal tools, chains, spikes, and rings. Quarrymen and stonemasons worked on the raw limestone with dolomite (a hard stone) cutting tools and iron chisels. Blacksmiths fabricated metal hand tools with brick furnaces, leather bellows, and hammers. Carpenters used special types of saws for different cuttings. One type, shown in Figure 3-3, consisted of a wood frame with a cord that kept a metal blade tight and straight. The cord was tightened with a wood tourniquet. In another type of saw, the blade was at the center. Herod's craftsmen laid out their work with measuring sticks, plumb bobs, and squares. They had bow drills to cut holes and used adzes (see Figure 3-4) to smooth their work. They pounded nails, spikes, and wooden dowels with hammers and mallets. Figure 3-5 is a Roman depiction of common tools used during that time.

There were several types of bow drills used. Figure 3-6 shows a wooden bow connected at the ends by a loose cord. The artisan placed a wooden shaft at the midpoint of the bow and wrapped the cord around it. When he moved the bow sidewise, the cord rotated the shaft, which had an iron point fitted to its lower end. A shaped stone socket held the upper end. The workman spun the bow drill by holding the bow with one hand and the stone guide socket with the other hand. This type of tool was used to bore holes ¼ to 4 inches in diameter in stone, the smaller point for granite and the larger for limestone.

Stonecutters and masons carved and dressed stone blocks with hard stone balls, combed chisels, and dentated scrapers. Most of these hand tools were made of hard dolomite stone. Figure 3-7 shows an artisan using a chisel to carve an Ionic capital. The Bible mentions such tools when describing how Solomon's

Figure 3-3
Typical handsaw

Figure 3-4
An adze

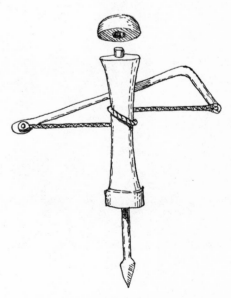

Figure 3-6
Bow drill

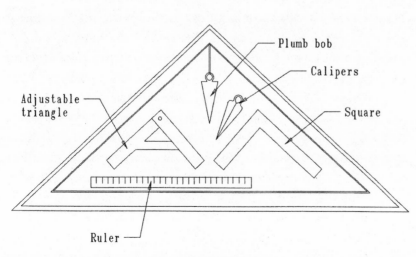

Figure 3-5
Typical hand tools, from a Roman inscription

Figure 3-7
Shaping an Ionic capital with a chisel

Figure 3-8
Biblical surveyors

Figure 3-9
Surveyors at work

workers prepared some of the large stones used for his public works projects in Jerusalem:

> All of these were of costly stones, according to the measures of hewn stones, sawed with saws, within and without, even from the foundation unto the coping, and so on the outside unto the great court. (1 Kings 7:9)

Herod's craftsmen used many kinds of measuring devices for precision work. They scribed circles and arcs with compasses, laid out distances with measuring rods and linen cords, and established right angles with squares. They controlled vertical and horizontal lines with plumb bobs and levels. Figures 3-8 and 3-9 show survey teams at work.

In Ezekiel's vision of the Temple, he describes a surveyor and his tools:

> And he brought me thither, and, behold, there was a man, whose appearance was like the appearance of brass, with a line of flax in his hand; and a measuring reed; . . . And behold a wall on the outside of the house round about, and in the man's hand a measuring reed of six cubits long, of a cubit and a handbreadth each; so he measured the breadth of the building, one reed, and the height, one reed. (Ezek. 40: 3–5)

Like modern surveyors, Herod's surveyors *staked out* level planes, lines, and right angles with *gromas* and *chorobates.* The groma was a portable four-foot-long wooden pole with a pair of cross arms rigidly attached to the top. Strings suspended from the ends of the arms carried weights. When the surveyor held the groma so that the strings were parallel to the pole, he knew the cross arms were horizontal. He then could sight across the top of either cross arm to establish a level plane or line. Figure 3-10 shows such a device.

The chorobate, useful for topographic surveying, was similar to the modern surveyor's plane table. It consisted of a wooden board with four rigidly braced legs fixed at right angles to the tabletop. Four strings with weights hung from the corners of the tabletop. When the surveyor observed that the strings were parallel to the table's legs, he knew the tabletop was horizontal. As a further check, he poured water into a narrow trough cut into the tabletop. If the water surface remained parallel to the top edge of the groove, it confirmed that the table was level. He could then sight across the tabletop to a measuring rod to set differences in elevation.

24

Machines and Engines

Vitruvius distinguished *machines* from *engines*. He wrote that machines required manpower or animal power while engines depended on potential or stored energy. For example, a crane for lifting heavy loads was a machine, whereas a catapult was an engine. Most machines used in construction were a combination of wood framing, pulley blocks, ropes, winches, hardware, and a means of applying force.

Figure 3-10
Groma, a surveyor's level

Transporting Stone Blocks

Some of the stone blocks in the Temple Mount walls weighed over 500 tons. Transporting and placing these immense weights required rigging, gin poles, ropes, hooks, pulleys, hoists, and knowledge of physical laws.

Workers on the Temple Mount used methods similar to those for loading and unloading ships. Figure 3-11 shows an aerial view of the harbor at Caesarea. Skilled riggers came to Jerusalem from Caesarea to lend their skills to the local builders. Figure 3-12 shows a typical Mediterranean merchant ship with a single mast, square sail, yardarm, and rope rigging.

Aristotle wrote many treatises on rollers and rolling friction. He also described how to split stone with wooden wedges. Figure 3-13 shows how workers moved heavy loads on wooden

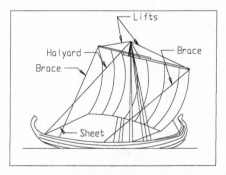

Figure 3-12
Typical Mediterranean merchant ship

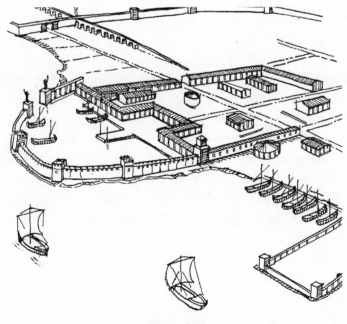

Figure 3-11
Harbor at Caesarea

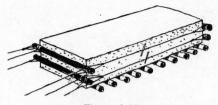

Figure 3-13
Transporting a large
stone block on rollers

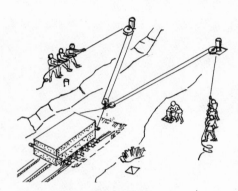

Figure 3-14
Moving a stone block with pulleys

rollers. Figure 3-14 illustrates how to use pulley blocks, slings, and capstans.

Other authorities were Philo, a Hellenistic engineer, Plutarch, and Hero, a mathematician. These wise men described how the system of counterweights, ropes, and pulley blocks could be used to lift heavy objects. They wrote about how to build a ship's mast and rigging, and about the mechanical advantage obtained by the windlass, lever, compound pulleys, wedge, worm, and gear trains. Hero derived the rule "work equals force times distance."

Scaffolding

The Second Temple was to be over 100 feet high. Carpenters erected wooden posts, spliced them end to end, tied cross beams with ropes, and dug holes in the ground to anchor the posts. They used wooden ladders to reach the various scaffold levels.

Ropes

For thousands of years, fiber ropes were the basic tools of mariners and riggers. The ancient Egyptians used ropes for moving and placing heavy stone blocks in the pyramids. In addition, ropemaking was important for ships that sailed along the Nile River and in the Mediterranean Sea.

Ropes were made of strong, flexible plant fibers such as sisal, jute, and hemp. Even the hairy outer covering of coconuts was a good ropemaking material. Raw plant fibers were first soaked, beaten, and combed in a bed of tall spikes, until they were converted into long, hairlike threads. These were spun together by hand to form yarns, which were gathered in loose skeins, preventing them from tangling. The skeins were twisted into bunches, forming strands. The strands were then twisted in opposite direction to its fibers to make a rope. This final twisting prevented the rope from unraveling. Figure 3-15 shows ropemakers at work. The manufacture of ropes required a lot of room, because the rope was woven in a straight, continuous line. A continuous rope was much stronger than one made up of pieces. Also, tarring the fiber ropes protected them from rotting when wet.

The Egyptians made enormous ropes, or *hawsers,* out of palm fiber and reeds. They used these hawsers to tie the ship's stem and stern together, in place of a keel. When twisted, the hawser formed a tourniquet of tremendous force that greatly stiffened the hull (see Figure 3-16).

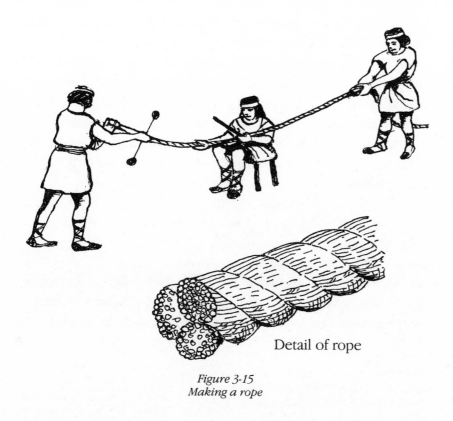

Detail of rope

Figure 3-15
Making a rope

The Persians also spun large-diameter ropes, some as long as a mile. Their military engineers used these large ropes to build the floating invasion bridges across the Hellespont.

Tarred fiber ropes were also used on ships to hold dolomite stone anchors. Seamen wrapped the line around a capstan mounted on the ship's deck. Then crewmen rotated the capstan with long poles to hoist the anchor from the sea bottom.

Herod's craftsmen studied the use of ropes on Egyptian, Phoenician, Greek, and Roman ships. They paid special attention to the rigging, pulleys, and hardware used to withstand the immense forces on the sails and handling of heavy cargo.

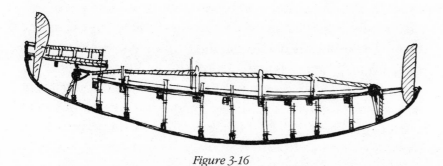

Figure 3-16
A hauser rope on an Egyptian ship

Although ropemakers could weave ropes as large as 8 inches in diameter, the diameter of pulleys and capstans and the ability of riggers to tie knots limited the size of the rope. The largest rope practical for use in construction of the Temple Mount was about 2 inches in diameter. The approximate breaking strength of a 1-inch-diameter fiber rope was about 7,000 pounds, and of a 2-inch rope it was approximately 10,000 pounds. Riggers knew from experience that friction and the age of the rope reduced its strength.

Herod's riggers understood that although a new rope had great strength, it could lose most of that strength through abrasion, mildew, and mistreatment. Therefore, the head rigger examined a rope carefully before using it, and he handled it properly. They did not allow dragging ropes over rough, rocky soil or storing a wet rope, which could cause mildew and deterioration. Riggers coiled and stored ropes on wooden racks above the ground or hung them from wooden pegs on walls.

Figure 3-17
Lifting a stone block with a pulley

Block and Tackle

A simple machine can multiply human strength. Nobody knows who invented the *block and tackle,* but many ancient societies used ropes and pulleys to lift heavy weights, as shown on Figure 3-17. Mariners used block and tackle for lifting and tightening heavy sails to the masts and yardarms and for handling cargo.

Figure 3-18 shows a hardwood pulley block with a single axle and double sheave (pulleys). Some pulley blocks housed two or more axles, each with its own set of sheaves. By the end of the Hellenistic age, block and tackle systems contained multiple pulleys for different rope sizes.

To pull heavy stone blocks across the ground, the workers anchored one pulley block to a wooden pile driven into the ground and the second to the block. They reeved, or strung, the rope between the two pulley blocks and pulled the end, either by men, oxen, or a capstan. The number of pulleys used amplified the pull on the rope. For example, five ropes reeved between the two pulley blocks increased the force at the end of the rope almost fivefold. Before lifting a heavy stone block, the rigger figured its weight, then selected the size and number of ropes needed to carry that load. Then he chose the number of blocks and size of pulleys. Finally, the rigger determined how to pull the rope.

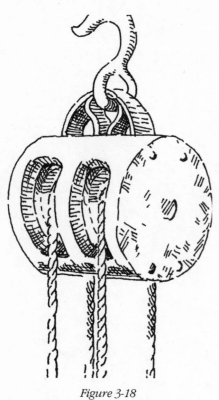

Figure 3-18
Wooden pulley block

Reeving, shown in Figure 3-19, is the form of multiple pulleys

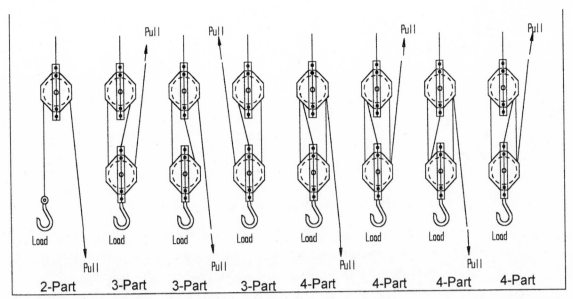

| 2-Part | 3-Part | 3-Part | 3-Part | 4-Part | 4-Part | 4-Part | 4-Part |

Figure 3-19
Block and tackle reeving

and ropes required for lifting a heavy load. For example, a rope over a single pulley would require an 800-pound pull to hold an 800-pound load. The same pull could hold 1,600 pounds in a two-part reeving, and approximately 2,400 pounds in a three-part reeving. Some of the force is lost, however, in friction between the rope and the sheaves.

The riggers used metal hardware to reduce wear on their ropes. These included iron hooks, forceps, rings, and shackles. When lifting stone blocks with rope slings, they placed padding at the corners of the blocks to protect the rope. Some riggers attached ropes without hardware but with intricate knotting. They used knots to anchor ends of rope, to extend or shorten ropes, and to tie ropes to structural members.

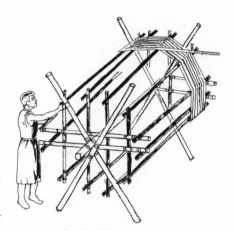

Figure 3-20
Horizontal capstan

Capstans, Winches, and Treadwheels

The riggers selected the method of pulling the rope. Teams of men required a lot of space. Oxen were stronger than men but were difficult to coordinate. The most efficient way of pulling a rope was found to be winding the rope around a capstan.

A capstan, commonly used to lift ship's anchors, consisted of a vertical drum which was rotated by means of handspikes, or long wooden poles. On land it was used to drag heavy stones. Teams of men pulled the hand poles as shown in Figure 3-20.

The Romans hoisted loads with large treadwheels (Figure 3-21). These were similar to waterwheels, in which the flowing

Figure 3-21
Roman treadwheel

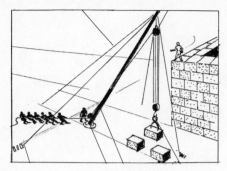

Figure 3-22
Lifting a stone block with a ginpole

water rotated the wheel. The treadwheel was wide enough to allow one or more men inside to continuously climb the rungs. Their weight rotated the wheel and drum, thereby exerting the pulling force. A 160-pound man climbing a 20-foot-diameter treadwheel rotating around a 2-foot-diameter axle could produce a pull of about 1,600 pounds, or ten times the man's weight. Increasing the number of men in the wheel magnified the pull proportionately.

Derricks and Cranes

Herod's carpenters erected many forms of cranes and derricks by using a combination of poles, beams, ropes, and pulleys. The wood for the cranes came from pine trees of Lebanon.

The simplest crane was a single inclined pole, called a *ginpole,* shown in Figure 3-22. By releasing and tightening the various *guy lines,* the riggers could rotate, raise, or lower the ginpole. A variation of this device was an inclined pole (boom) attached to the bottom of a vertical pole (mast), as illustrated in Figure 3-23. The boom rotated, raised or lowered as required to position the load.

Another type of crane was the A-frame crane. It consisted of two inclined poles set up as an inverted "V." These devices were crude, but easy to build and use. Figures 3-24 and 3-25 show

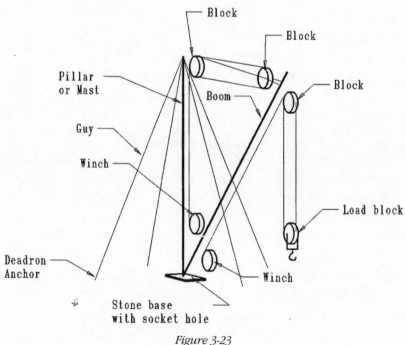

Figure 3-23
A ginpole derrick

30

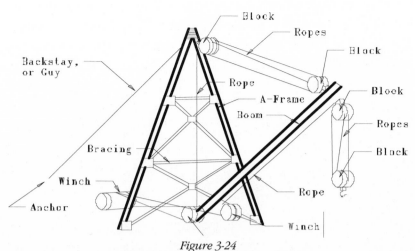

Figure 3-24
Using an A-frame derrick to load a block

A-frame derricks. Figure 3-26 depicts a stiff-leg derrick. To keep the crane stable, riggers braced it in three or four directions with rope guys anchored to the ground with pegs. They tied a pulley to the top of the frame and reeved the rope through another pulley that held a hook. They pulled the rope by manpower, winches, or capstans. They anchored the mast into a shaped stone socket set in the ground. Although a wooden A-frame was strong enough to lift 50 tons, the size of rope, number of pulleys, and means of applying force limited its lifting capacity.

The riggers used cranes and derricks for placing heavy stone lintels over doorways, as shown in Figure 3-27. They also used this equipment to erect wood roof framing and stone walls. This work required great skill, since improper use could damage the dressed building blocks or cause serious injury or death.

In summary, building the Temple Mount required many types of derricks, including the following:

- A *ginpole derrick* consisted of a mast with guys from its top, arranged to permit the mast to lean in any direction. The load was raised or lowered by ropes leading through pulley blocks at the top of the mast.
- A *fixed or guyed derrick* was similar to the ginpole derrick except that the mast rotated. Three or more guys supported the mast in a vertical position. A boom, pivoted at the bottom, moved in a vertical plane. Rope lines between the head of the mast and the end of the boom raised and lowered the boom. Rope lines from the end of the boom raised and lowered the load.

31

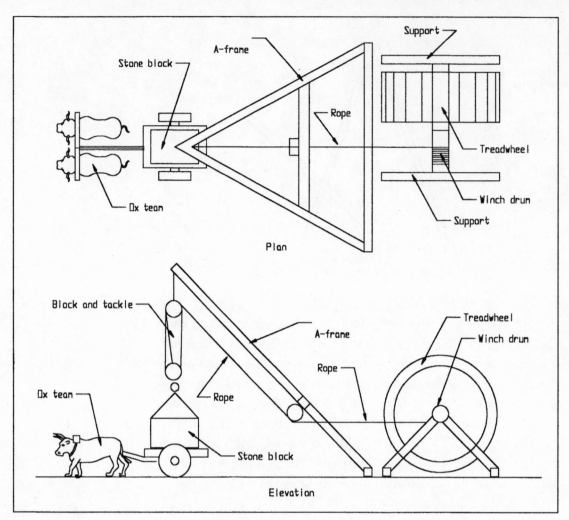

Figure 3-25
Using an A-frame for
raising a stone block

- A *stiff-leg derrick* was similar to the guyed derrick except that two or more poles supported the mast. Each pole could resist pulling or pushing forces. There were usually timber sills, or ties, connecting the lower ends of the stiff legs to the foot of the mast.

- A *breast derrick without a boom* consisted of a mast constructed of two side members, upright posts that were spread at their base. Rigid wooden struts tied the two side members together at the top and bottom. Guys held the top to prevent tipping. Ropes through a pulley block secured to the crosspiece raised or lowered the load.

- The *A-frame derrick* consisted of a tower made of two masts spread apart at the bottom and connected at the top. A boom, hinged from a cross member spread between the bottom ends of the two upright members, lifted the load. The upper end of

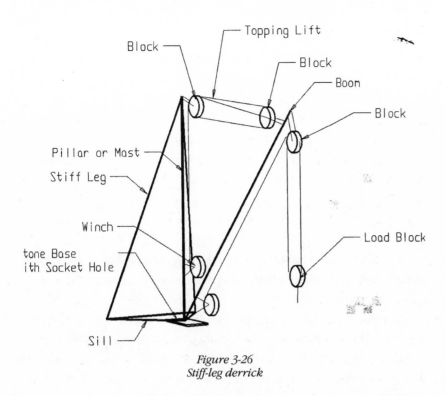

Figure 3-26
Stiff-leg derrick

the boom was secured to the upper junction of the side members. Wooden timbers braced the upright members, guyed from their apex to the ground.

- A *shear* was a simple A-frame structure made of two poles connected at the top and spread apart at their bases. Guy ropes supported the apex of the frame. Riggers used these frames with a winch or block and tackle to raise and lower loads.

Rigging

Engineers and riggers working on the Temple Mount project had to know mathematics. To calculate the forces involved in lifting a load, they used a graphical analysis. They also used the abacus to calculate the volume and weight of the stone blocks, as well as its center of gravity in order to prevent tipping or rotating.

Figure 3-28 shows one way they used hooks to lift stone blocks. Another way was to leave projections on opposite sides of the stone block for rope attachment. Another was to insert iron wedges into holes cut into the top face of the blocks. Yet another method was to cut slots into the sides of the block for rope slings or iron tongs.

Levers

Archimedes once said, "Give me a long enough pole, a fulcrum, and a place to stand, and I will move the world."

The builders moved stone blocks onto sleds or into a wall with levers. A lever simply magnifies the force applied on an object. One early form of the lever was the Egyptian *shadoof.* It consists of a counterweighted long bar pivoted near one end, enabling a farmer to lift a bucket of water from the Nile River into an irrigation ditch.

Herod's workers used an iron bar as a lever to lift stone blocks. They set the end of the bar under the edge of the block, then placed the bar on a hardwood block fulcrum and lifted the block. In this way much less effort needed to be applied to the other end of the bar.

They used a rotating platform to raise stone columns. Riggers first tied the column down to a horizontal frame attached to a wooden tower. Then they rotated the assembly with the column. When the tower was horizontal, the column was in a vertical position, and they then lowered the column to rest on a prepared stone foundation.

Pile Drivers

Woodpiles were very important to ancient engineers, not only for supporting foundations but also to anchor ropes and pulleys. Some pile anchors consisted of poles lashed to cross members. These were placed into excavated trenches and backfilled with rocks and sand. Figure 3-29 shows a typical pile anchor tied to a capstan. The piles were driven into the ground manually or mechanically, in one of the following ways:

- The *hand ram,* shown in Figure 3-30, consisted of a small platform for workers mounted near the top of the pile. The workers lifted and dropped a heavy iron *mandrel* that slid over an iron post extended above the top of the pile. The mandrel struck the post, thereby impacting the pile and driving it into the ground.
- Pile driving with a *maul* (see Figure 3-31) consisted of a temporary platform placed near the top of the pile. The workers alternately would hammer the pile with a heavy maul.
- Pile driving with a mandrel was similar to the action of battering rams. Vitruvius described this in his *Book Ten Chapter XV 5.* It consisted of a beak of iron mounted on a long wooden arm.

Figure 3-27
Setting a stone lintel

Figure 3-28
Lifting a stone block with a hook

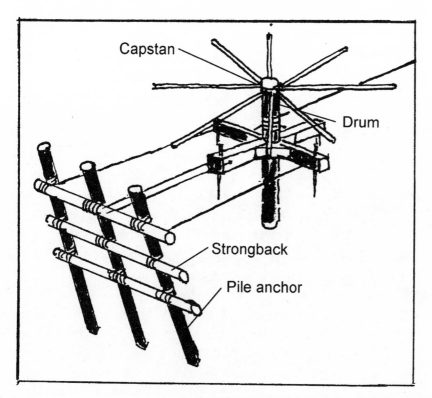

Figure 3-29
Anchor and capstan

From the head to the heel of the beam were iron chains suspended from a framework of wood uprights and cross pieces. As the heel of the arm was pulled down, the ram was lifted. When the arm was released, the ram struck the pile with great force, as shown in Figure 3-32. Like the battering ram, the pile driver could be taken apart and moved to new locations.

- The *ratchet-winch ram* consisted of an A-frame that supported an iron ram suspended from a pulley. The rope that suspended the ram extended over a pulley and then to a ratchet-winch. As the winch was rotated by hand, the rope lifted the ram. After the ram was lifted 4 or 5 feet, it was released and fell on the pile.

- The *hand-operated machine maul* was used to drive a batter or sloping pile. A heavy maul was attached to a long wooden arm pivoted from a frame. Workers pulled the opposite end of the lever down to lift the maul. Then they released the arm and the maul swung down in its arc, striking the pile.

- The *treadwheel-operated pile driver* was an alternate for the winch. When the treadwheel was rotated, the hammer rose and fell as a tripping device released it.

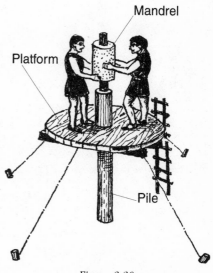

Figure 3-30
Driving a pile with a hand ram

Figure 3-31
Driving a pile with a maul

The type of pile used depended on the soil condition. A soft soil over bedrock required an end-bearing pile. When a dense soil was encountered, friction-type piles were used. Battered piles were required to resist horizontal and uplift forces. Pairs of battered piles were very effective anchors for guy lines, winches, and capstans.

Where workers encountered rocky soil, they cut a hole and set the pile into it; then they filled the space around the pile with a mixture of water, cement, sand, and asphalt. Sometimes they reinforced the piles with lagging.

PART 2 TRANSPORTATION

The Holy Land was the hub of many caravan routes between Europe, Asia, and Africa. The shortest access between the Mediterranean Sea and the Red Sea was across Palestine. Conquering armies from Egypt, Babylon, and Rome had to use this land to expand their influence and commerce. This movement of manpower and material created a need for effective transportation.

The earliest method was by caravan, which did not need good roadways. Camels and asses *(onagers)* (Figure 3-33) traveled on sandy and rocky land, since they had the ability to avoid obsta-

36

A-frame

Maul

Piles

Figure 3-32
Driving piles with a maul from an A-frame

cles. The amount of cargo carried was limited only by the number of draft animals available. Donkeys were used to augment manpower. Donkeys and mules were preferred for carrying heavy loads over great distances. As a pack animal, a mule had several advantages over the horse. It was more amenable to the task of carrying a load and, being less temperamental, it was easier to train.

The Roman soldiers recognized this fact when they called themselves *Marius' mules,* after being required during the Marius' reforms of 101 BCE to carry with patience heavier equipment on route marches than they normally carried (Frontinus, Strategemata IV, 7).

Draft Animals

An ox is a full-grown castrated bull. Although unattractive and slower than a horse, it could be fed cheaply and was able to pull as much as could two horses of comparable size. Certain types of cattle were bred to produce large, powerful oxen for draft animals.

The main advantage of a horse over an ox was speed. This was important in warfare and chariot racing. A horse could carry about one-ninth of its weight per day traveling 2.5 miles per

Figure 3-33
Transporting a log by donkey

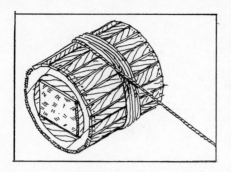

Figure 3-34
Rolling a stone block

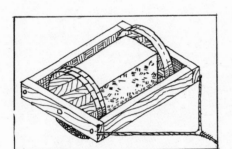

Figure 3-35
Moving a stone block

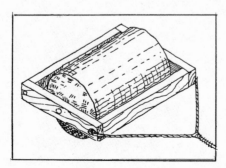

Figure 3-36
Rolling a stone cylinder

hour. A 1,000-pound horse could exert about three-quarter horsepower.

The shape of the ox, with its minor hump at the withers, lent itself to the yoke. The harness kept the yoke in place. Yoking was not efficient for the horse's shape. In some places, shafts that ran beside the animal and lower down than the yoke replaced the yoke and pole. A stiff collar that did not ride up the neck, but put pressure on the shoulders and chest of the horse, replaced the flexible throat-harness used on the oxen. At the same time, the shafts ensured equal pull on both sides.

Because these draft animals were such an important part of the economy in biblical times, the Bible itself contains various regulations regarding their use and treatment. Here are two examples from the Book of Deuteronomy:

Thou shalt not plow with an ox and an ass together. (Deut. 22:10)
Thou shalt not muzzle the ox when he treadeth out the corn. (Deut. 25:4)

In addition, Exodus 21:28–36 and Deuteronomy 22:1–4 contain further provisions regarding an owner's responsibility for his animals as well as the animals of other members of the community.

Rollers, Rails, and Sleds

During the construction of the Temple Mount, one of the major limestone quarries was about 125 feet higher than the work site. A temporary mile-long roadway along the Tyropoeon Valley was built between the higher quarry and the building site.

The amount of manpower needed to pull a heavy stone or a sled was related to the steepness of the slope and the friction between the sled and the ground. Workers used water, milk, or oil to lubricate the ground, or they embedded logs in the earth. They moved the heavier stone blocks on sleds or rolled them. These methods are shown in Figures 3-34, 3-35, 3-36, 3-37, and 3-38. Figure 3-39 shows another method used to move a stone block.

It took eight men to move a seven-ton stone block on a level grade, but more men were required to pull it uphill. An ancient Egyptian illustration depicted 172 men pulling a 60-ton statue on a sled without rollers. To build the pyramids, they dragged gran-

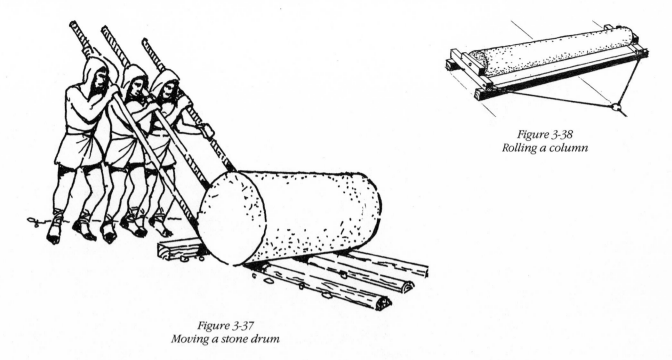

Figure 3-38
Rolling a column

Figure 3-37
Moving a stone drum

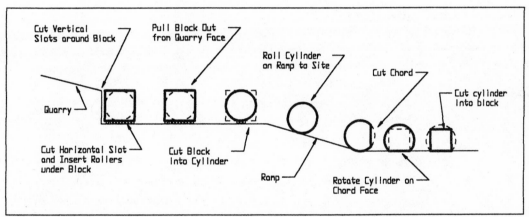

Figure 3-39
Chord method for moving stone blocks

ite stone blocks up earthen ramps. Hundreds of workers constructed these ramps with over a million tons of sand. Afterwards they removed and redistributed it back over the desert.

To build the Temple Mount walls, teams of men, oxen, or capstans pulled wooden sleds carrying stone blocks with ropes. Figures 3-40 and 3-41 show 12-ox and 32-ox teams pulling stone blocks. Workers also used wooden sleds with rounded bottoms. To place the block, they tipped the sled on its side.

Wheeled Vehicles

In order to administer their kingdoms effectively, kings in the ancient world needed to have effective means of transportation at

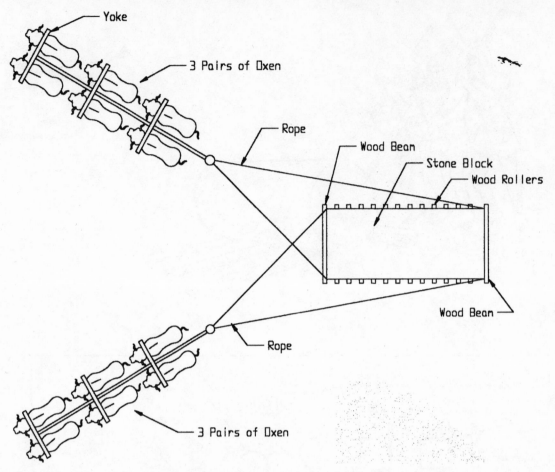

Figure 3-40
12 oxen pulling a stone block

their disposal. Travel between towns would have been difficult without wheeled vehicles. The Bible describes two of the more successful kings of ancient Israel, Solomon and Hezekiah, as having an extensive array of horses and chariots:

> And Solomon had forty thousand stalls of horses for his chariots, and twelve thousand horsemen (1 Kings 5:6)
> And Hezekiah had exceeding much riches and honor; and he provided him . . . stalls for all manners of beasts, and flocks in folds . . . he provided him . . . possessions of flocks and herds in abundance. (2 Chron. 32:27–29)

In addition, because many important trading routes passed through ancient Israel, Solomon was able to enrich himself and his kingdom through an extensive trade in horses and chariots.

> And Solomon gathered chariots and horsemen; and he had a thousand and four hundred chariots, and twelve thousand

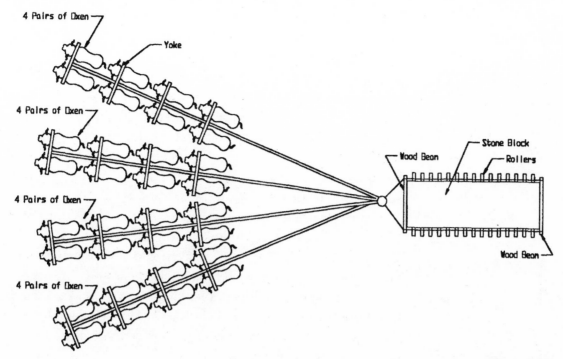

Figure 3-41
32 oxen pulling a stone block

horsemen, that he placed in the chariot cities, and with the king at Jerusalem. And the king made silver and gold to be in Jerusalem as stones, and cedars made he to be as the sycamore-trees that are in the Lowland, for abundance. And the horses which Solomon had were brought out of Egypt; also out of Keve, the king's merchants buying them of the men of Keve at a price. And they fetched up, and brought out of Egypt a chariot for six hundred shekels of silver, and a horse for a hundred and fifty; and so for all the kings of the Hittites, and the kings of Aram, did they bring them out by their means. (2 Chron. 1:14–17)

Figure 3-42
Moving a stone block by manpower

Thus Solomon bought chariots from Egypt and animals from Asia for export to Hittite and Aramean kings. Royal stables in Megiddo contained rows of stone columns that divided plastered fodder troughs for the animals.

Vehicle development started with logs placed under heavy stone blocks pulled by men as shown in Figure 3-42. They continuously moved the logs from the rear to the front of the load, setting timber rails in the path in order to provide a relatively smooth surface. Figure 3-43 shows men pulling an obelisk, and Figure 3-44 illustrates how they erected a large obelisk with a ramp.

Figure 3-43
Pulling an obelisk

41

Figure 3-44
Raising an obelisk with a ramp

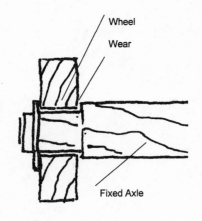

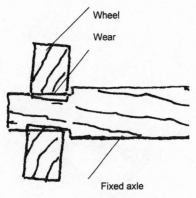

Figure 3-45
Types of axles

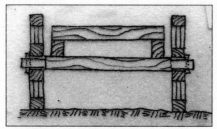

Figure 3-46
Fixed axle and rotating wheel

Later, ancient cartwrights cut logs to form crude wheels and mounted them on ends of wooden axles, as shown in Figure 3-45. They placed wooden beams across the axles, forming a platform for cargo. Figures 3-46 and 3-47 show two methods of attaching a wheel to an axle.

Wheel construction improved from a single slice to sections of logs. The center and outer segments of the wheel were shaped from these sections. The three segments were locked together by metal straps, spikes, and metal rims. The rims protected the softer wood from abrasion and wear.

To provide a better wearing surface and to lock sections of the wheel together, they expanded an iron rim by heat and placed it around the wheel. When the metal cooled, it contracted, tightly holding sections of the wheel together.

The Philistines developed a simple cart with a wood-framed box mounted upon an axle with two wooden wheels. However, they used carts only for transporting property and not for military purposes, as did the Canaanites.

The carrying capacity and speed of the carts depended mainly on the type of wheels. In time, wheels became lighter and more durable. A lighter spoked wheel provided the speed and maneuverability needed by the chariots. See Figure 3-48. A linchpin is used to prevent a wheel from falling off. A nave is a thick piece in the center of a wheel into which spokes and axle are inserted. It's also called a hub.

The chariot (Figure 3-49) was a mobile firing platform. In addition to its agility, it had few parts—a body, wheels, pole, yoke, and axle—and two men could carry them over rough terrain. In battle, they fitted the chariot with quivers, bow cases, sheaths, and spear stands.

At the height of the Assyrian imperial power in the eighth to seventh century BCE, their chariot corps was the most powerful striking force in the world. Their vehicles had large wheels capable of carrying the body of the chariot loaded with four warriors: a driver, an archer, and two shield bearers. These were awesome war machines. In addition, cavalry archers on horseback protected the charioteers. In Babylon, carving out portions of the wood between the rim and the hub provided a sculptured, lighter wheel. In Egypt, leather thongs tied the rim to the wheel.

More efficient wheeled vehicles required a better network of roads, which in turn expanded trade throughout the Mediterranean. In addition, armies benefited because they could travel farther and faster to conquer larger territories.

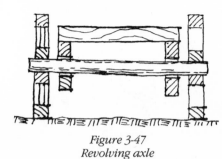

Figure 3-47
Revolving axle

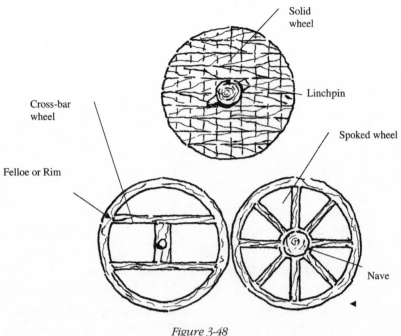

Figure 3-48
Types of ancient wooden wheels

Nonmilitary vehicles fell into two categories: ox-drawn farm wagons and the lighter, horse-drawn carriages to transport passengers. Two animals drew most wagons, since the method of attaching them was by yoke and pole. Ox-drawn wagons preceded the horse-drawn ones. Figure 3-50 shows a four-ox team pulling a wagon carrying a large stone block.

Platforms were mounted on either one or two axles. Oxen usually drew the two-wheeled carts, with the load balanced over the single axle, since an unbalanced loaded cart would tend to tip (see figure 3-51). Oxen were better able to cope with the weight pushing down on the yoke or with an upward pull on the girth-strap.

The wheels were fixed to axles that rotated within brackets fastened to the cart's frame, or the wheels rotated about fixed axles. See Figure 3-52. On lighter vehicles, the axle was fixed and the wheels turned on a short stub at each end. A *linchpin* passing through the stub prevented the wheel from coming off. A metal washer separated the hub of the wheel from the linchpin to prevent excessive wear.

Major technological developments of the wagon occurred during Roman times. One was the pivoted front axle. This invention allowed a wagon to turn more easily. In addition, they no longer needed the single pole yoke that required two draft ani-

Figure 3-49
A chariot body

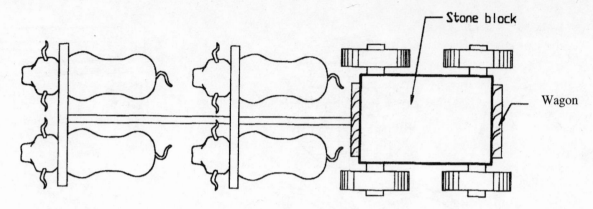

Figure 3-50
Four-ox team with wagon

Figure 3-51
Pair of oxen pulling a cart with a block

> . . . *And as he promised them this beforehand, so he did not break his word with them, but got ready a thousand wagons, that were to bring stones for the building, and chose out ten thousand of the most skillful workmen, and bought a thousand sacerdotal garments for as many of the priests, and had some of them taught the arts of stone cutters, and others of carpenters, and then began to build; but this not till everything was prepared for the work. . . . (Josephus, Ant Book XV Chapter XI)*

mals. A pair of parallel shafts permitting one draft animal replaced the single pole. The Romans also developed the suspended carriage, which softened the bumps and jolts caused by a rough terrain. This innovation also reduced the stress on the axle, undercarriage, and fragile cargo.

Vitruvius described how to install an *odometer* on carriages, to record the distance traversed. This description of the odometer appeared in Book X of the *Ten Books of Architecture* as follows:

1. Let the wheels of a carriage be each four feet in diameter, so that if a wheel has a mark made upon it, and begins to move forward from that mark in making its revolution on the surface of the road, it will have covered a definite distance of twelve and some half feet on reaching that mark at which it began to revolve. . . .

2. Having provided such wheels, let a drum with a single tooth projecting beyond the surface be firmly fastened to the inner side of the hub of the wheel. Then above this let a case be firmly fastened to the body of the carriage, containing a revolving drum set on an edge and mounted on an axle; on the face of the drum there are four hundred teeth, placed at equal intervals and engaging the tooth of the drum below. The up-

per drum has, moreover, one tooth fixed to its side and standing out farther than the other teeth.

3. Then, above, let there be a horizontal drum, similarly toothed and contained in another case, with its teeth engaging the tooth fixed to the side of the second drum, and let as many holes are made in this (third) drum as will correspond to the number of miles—more or less—that a carriage can go in a day's journey. Let a small round stone be placed in every one of these holes, and in a receptacle or case containing that drum let one hole be made, with a small pipe attached, through which, when they reach that point, the stones placed in the drum may fall one by one into a bronze vessel set underneath in the body of the carriage.

4. Thus, as the wheel in going forward carries with it the lowest drum, and as the tooth of this at every revolution strikes against the teeth of the upper drum, and makes it move along, the result will be that the upper drum is carried round once every four hundred revolutions of the lowest, and that the tooth fixed to its side pushes forward one tooth of the horizontal drum. Since there are four hundred revolutions in the lowest drum, the upper will revolve once, the progress made will be a distance of five thousand feet or one mile. Hence, every stone, making a ringing sound as it falls, will give warning that we have gone one mile. The number of stones gathered and counted will show the number of miles in a day's journey. (Morris Hicky Morgan, trans.)

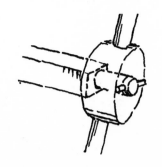

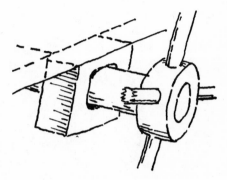

Figure 3-52
Hubs for fixed and revolving axles

Josephus wrote that a thousand two-wheel and four-wheel carts were built to transport stone from the quarries to the Temple Mount (Ant 15:390). A pair of oxen pulled each two-wheel cart, and four oxen pulled each four-wheel cart. The wheels were solid, built up of two semicircles of wood. Bronze and iron rims protected the wood from wear.

Although the load that a cart carried was important, the amount of pull required to start moving was even more critical. When the wheels of a cart begin to roll, there was a reaction (rolling resistance) by the roadway opposite to the direction of rolling. The amount of rolling resistance depended on the type of wheel and the roadway surface.

Herod's teamsters found that the rolling resistance of wooden wheels on soft ground was greater than on hard ground or than wheels with iron rims. Therefore, they preferred large wooden wheels with iron rims and a roadway surface of embedded tim-

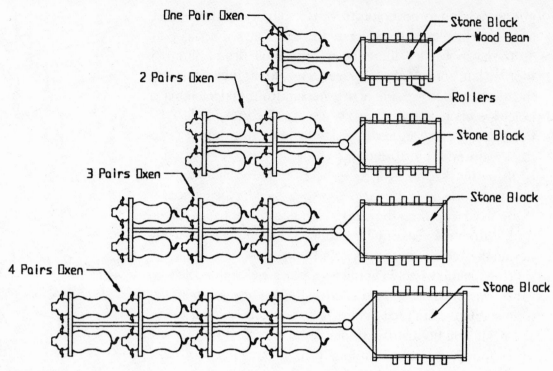

Figure 3-53
Ox teams pulling stone blocks

bers. This combination reduced the rolling resistance and made pulling easier.

For hauling very heavy loads, teams of oxen were lined up in tandem to pull a single rope. Sometimes four or more ropes were fastened to a single stone block and each rope was drawn by many pairs of oxen. In this way, stone blocks weighing as much as 500 tons could be moved. Figure 3-53 illustrates one to four pairs of ox teams.

Manpower

In the ancient world, most manpower came not from slaves, but from the corvée system. This was a system of forced labor imposed by a ruler over his subjects that was commonly employed when large building projects were undertaken. It could also be described as a system of taxation that citizens paid through labor rather than money or goods. In ancient times, as is reflected in the Bible, one dominant ethnic group would often impose corvée labor upon another. We can see such examples with Egypt and the Israelites (Exod. 1:8–15) and with the Israelites and the Canaanites (Judges 1:28, 30, 33, 35 and possibly in Joshua 9:21, where the Gibeonites are made into "hewers of wood and drawers of water"). When Solomon began to construct the Temple in Jerusalem, the Bible says that he conscripted labor from "all of Israel" (1 Kings 5:27), but it is possible that these laborers were taken mainly from the Canaanite population and not from among the Israelites (1 Kings 9:15–22).

Labor by women was described by the poet Antipater of Thessalonica, who wrote in 100 BCE:

Cease from grinding, ye women of toil at the mill; sleep late, even if the crowing cocks announce the dawn. For Demater has ordered the Nymphs to perform the work of your hands, and they, leaping down on the top of the wheel, turn its axle which, with revolving spokes, turns the heavy concave Nisyrian millstones. (Archer, Fischler, Wyke)

Herod financed the work on the Temple Mount from taxes on citizens and tolls levied on passing caravans. Commerce traveled over many highways from the north, south, and east. Tolls were also collected at the ports of Caesarea, Acco, and Jaffa, which were used for export and import. The Jordan Valley was fertile and exported an abundance of agricultural products.

According to Josephus, ten thousand artisans, including a thousand priests, were to be put to work by Herod (Ant 15:390). The manpower for this project was so large that when the Temple Mount project was finally completed, there was great concern about the potential social problems arising from the 18,000 laborers in Jerusalem who would no longer be employed. As a result, according to Josephus, "make-work" public works projects were created to keep the laborers employed (Ant 20:219–222). Similar concerns may have led the Roman emperor Vespasian to forgo labor-saving devices, according to the following Roman record, for fear that unemployment would result:

An engineer offered to haul some huge columns up to the capitol at a moderate expense by a simple mechanical device, but Vespasian declined his services and saying, "I must always ensure that the working class earn enough money to buy themselves food." Nevertheless he paid the engineer a very handsome fee. (Duncan-Jones, 1982)

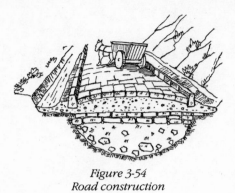

Figure 3-54
Road construction

The work on the Temple Mount started in 23 or 20 BCE (23 BCE according to War 1:401, and 20 BCE according to Ant 15:380). The Temple itself was completed in one and a half years (Ant 15:421), but work on other parts of the Temple Mount continued until 64 CE (Ant 20:219). Much of the work during these later years was undertaken to repair extensive damage that had occurred during a series of small revolts that broke out after Herod the Great's death, when there was some question as to which of his sons would succeed him (Ant 17:261–64; War 2:49-50). In all, it took approximately 46 years to build the Temple Mount (John 2:20).

Roadways

Paved roads existed in ancient Israel as early as the third millennium BCE, but only within urban areas. In the open areas between cities, for thousands of years road building consisted merely of clearing away boulders, moving them to the sides of the road, and filling in the larger holes. Transport of military siege engines and heavily laden supply wagons essential for war required better roadways, and the actual paving of highways between cities was introduced to the Near East by the Romans.

Some paved roads were processional ways, as in Nebuchadnezzar's Babylon. These roads were paved with limestone slabs placed over large flat bricks, which in turn were set in a mixture of lime, sand, and asphalt. During religious processions, wagons bearing statues of the gods had wheels. Some processional roadways had grooves in the pavement for the sacred wagons, in order to ensure a smooth, safe ride for the gods.

Ancient roads usually followed the beds of dry rivers and streams. Others were only a pair of ruts worn into the soil. Some of these ruts were lined with cut stone and split into switches and sidings like modern railroad tracks. Because the distance between the wheels varied, the ruts did not always fit the wheels of alien vehicles.

While Assyrian records do occasionally refer to the process of clearing out roadways to allow their troops and chariots to pass through, these roads were certainly not the extensive engineering feats later built by the Roman Empire. Figure 3-54 illustrates the construction of Roman roads, which have lasted over 2,000 years.

Local rulers maintained the roads from fees and tolls charged to travelers. It may be for this reason that a major transportation route along the Jordan River was known as the King's Highway (Num. 20:17). Josephus wrote that King Solomon paved roads leading to Jerusalem with black stones (Ant 8:187). This highway ran from On at the Nile River, north of Memphis, to Elath, to Hazor and Damascus, then northeast to Tadmor and east to Babylon and Ur on the Euphrates River. The *Via Maris Highway* extended from Zoan on the Nile Delta to Gaza, then to Megiddo, Hazor, Damascus, and Aleppo in Syria. East–west roads connected the cities on the Mediterranean to Nineveh, Assur, Dumah, and other cities in Iraq, Saudi Arabia, and Iran.

All major roads built during the Roman Period were paved, and milestones marked out distances between towns. Roman army engineers constructed and maintained these roads when not engaged in fighting or guard duty. This probably was the first civil engineering corps.

A vast road system of over 75,000 miles extended over the entire Roman Empire. Twenty-nine highways radiating from Rome interconnected with other roads. Many were paved with several layers of stone. The more important paved roads had a deep subbase of compacted rubble, overlain by strata of flat slabs. The stones were set in mortar; over a thick base of concrete and crushed rock the close-fitted stones were paved. Crowned pavement surfaces drained toward the curbstones that lined each side of the road. Drainage ditches carried away rainwater. Some roads were built with inverted crowns so that rainwater flowed toward the center of the roadway.

Road building between Judean towns was well developed by King Herod. He constructed a road grid system in Caesarea and a Roman forum at the intersection of the two principal streets. The street that led to the amphitheater was colonnaded on both sides. In Jerusalem, Tyropoleon Street was surfaced with great hewn slabs of limestone.

The biblical road-builders recognized the importance of good road design. Where possible, they built roads in a straight line. They made deep cuts and fills to smooth out excessive slopes, and they installed culverts and bridges over watercourses.

Ships and Harbors

Shipping was important to King Solomon for maintaining his commerce with the neighboring countries. The Holy Land lacked great forests, so timber had to be imported. When Solomon constructed the First Temple in Jerusalem, he imported much of the building materials and skilled labor from his Phoenician neighbor to the north, King Hiram of Tyre:

> [Solomon said to Hiram,] "Now therefore command thou that they hew me cedar-trees out of Lebanon; and my servants shall be with thy servants; and I will give thee hire for thy servants according to all that thou shalt say; for thou knowest that there is not among us any that hath skill to hew timber like unto the Zidonians." . . . [Hiram replied,] "My servants shall bring them down from Lebanon unto the sea; and I will make them into rafts to go by sea unto the place that thou shalt appoint me, and will cause them to be broken up there, and thou shalt receive them; and thou shalt accomplish my desire, in giving food for my household." So Hiram gave Solomon timber of cedar and timber of cypress according to all his desire . . . And he sent them [thirty thousand men] to Lebanon, ten thousand a month by courses: a month they were in Lebanon, and two months at home; and Adoniram was over the levy. . . . [as well as] three thousand and three hundred, who bore rule over the people that wrought in the work. . . . And Solomon's builders and Hiram's builders and the Gebalites did fashion them, and prepared the timber and the stones to build the house. (1 Kings 5:20, 23–24, 28–32)

In a parallel passage in 2 Chronicles, we get a glimpse of the wages that such skilled laborers could command:

> [Solomon said to Hiram,] "Send me also cedar-trees, cypress-trees, and sandal-wood, out of Lebanon; for I know that thy servants have skill to cut timber in Lebanon; and behold, my servants shall be with thy servants. . . . And, behold, I will give to thy servants, the hewers that cut timber, twenty thousand measures of beaten wheat, and twenty thousand measures of barley, and twenty thousand baths of wine, and twenty thousand baths of oil." (2 Chron. 2:7–9)

Merchant ships that could carry 1,300 tons of cargo or 600 passengers were up to 180 feet long, 65 feet wide, and 44 feet from the deck to the keel. For most ships, the ratio of length to width of the hull was 5½ to 6½.

Most ships had broad square sails made of lengths of linen cloth sewn together. Generally, the sails were white, although ships belonging to royalty had purple sails. Military ships had green-blue sails for camouflage. The shipbuilders reinforced the sails with leather brails (ties) and supported them from a mast and yardarm (cross arms). Basic equipment on a ship included two anchors with winches or capstans, lead lines to sound depth, mooring lines, and flags and lanterns for signaling.

In the fourth century BCE, Phoenician mariners sailed wooden ships for commerce along Palestine's Mediterranean coast. A typical ship was 37 feet long and 13 feet wide. It displaced about 20 tons, 12 tons of which was ballast. The ships were built with a keel along the lowest part of the hull, as well as stringers, stanchions, and planks. Oak mortise-and-tenon joints connected planks and wooden members. Structural components of the ship were made of pine except for the tenons and the false keel, which were dense oaks.

The shipwrights carved the ship's anchor and arm from a single oak timber and coated the arm's tooth with copper. They filled the stock with lead for weight. The skill of these ancient shipwrights carried over to the proficiency of the land-based carpenters.

Engineering in the Far East

Concurrent with the events in the Middle East and the Mediterranean, engineering was advancing in the Far East. Toward the end of the biblical period, people in the ancient Near East made many contacts with Chinese merchant ships and overland caravans.

The impact of China's science and technology was significant. During the Han dynasty in 138 BCE, Zhang Qian, a diplomatic envoy, blazed a trail to the Middle Eastern countries. When he went to the Western Regions, he traveled through Indoscythe (in Pakistan) and the northern section of Afghanistan. His travels also took him through Parthia (in Iran and Iraq). During this period, China and these countries freely exchanged envoys and merchants.

Chinese technology of smelting iron and digging wells spread. Chinese silk, iron, and steel were the most popular products shipped to Rome, in exchange for agricultural and art products.

One trade route extended from Changan (or Xian, capital of Western Han) to the eastern coast of the Mediterranean, a distance of more than 4,000 miles. This overland route connected Istanbul in Asia Minor, Antioch, and Tyre in Lebanon with the ancient capitals of Xian and Luoyang in China. It was the longest and most important land trade route in the ancient world. Since merchants used this road mostly for transporting silk from China, they called it the *Silk Road*.

Chinese seagoing ships, carrying Arabian traders, traveled along the coasts of Southeast Asia to the Red Sea and Eastern African ports. From very early times, people along the Mediterranean maintained commercial relations with India, Arabia, and China. From India came such luxuries as pearls, gems, and tortoise shells. Ships loaded at India's northwest ports sailed westward and turned up the Persian Gulf to discharge at its head. From there, camels took the merchandise to Seleuceia and then to the overland route. Another sea route bypassed India to sail directly into the Red Sea and then by caravan across the Arabian or Egyptian deserts to the Mediterranean.

Summary

King Herod's master builders combined the basic laws of physics with an abundance of raw materials, cheap labor, and time. They had the ability, opportunity, and incentive to construct the magnificent Temple Mount. The completed work won the admiration of the entire Mediterranean world.

CHAPTER 4

Engineering, Planning, and Logistics

During King Herod's reign, his engineers built roads, reservoirs, and aqueducts to improve Judean life. An easier lifestyle reduced the people's unrest and allowed Herod to govern less severely. Not only had the Judeans absorbed skills from the Babylonians and Phoenicians, they learned much from the Greek and Roman engineers as well. The Romans had inherited their building techniques from the Etruscans, who had previously ruled the Italian peninsula for 300 years. Each generation of engineers copied and improved on the methods of their predecessors and neighbors. This chapter will briefly describe some of the major figures of ancient engineering and what we know about their writings.

Vitruvius

Vitruvius, an important Roman engineer and philosopher, who was active during the latter part of the first century BCE, listed the requirements of a good engineer or architect as follows:

- He must be literate and able to express himself clearly.
- He must be a skilled draftsman, and capable of drawing plans, elevations, and renderings in perspective sketches.
- He must be a mathematician and also be competent in geometric construction and arithmetic.
- He must have an encyclopedic knowledge of mythology and legend, to plan sculptures and friezes for buildings.
- He must be familiar with several branches of philosophy.
- He must understand the basics of acoustics, musical theory, and medicine as these relate to public health.

- He must understand the laws concerning drainage rights and lighting.
- He must be able to prepare a contract that is clear and unambiguous and that will prevent litigation later.
- He must have enough knowledge of astronomy to work out the directions from the sun and stars and to calibrate sundials at different latitudes. (Landels)

Vitruvius wrote this in his ten volumes of *De Architectura* during the reign of Emperor Augustus. The term *Architectura* was from the Greek "craft organizer," or "a person who coordinates and directs the work of various craftsmen." He dedicated his books to the rebuilding of Rome after the Civil War, at the beginning of the Herodian Period. They contained the following information:

- Book I was an encyclopedia of knowledge required for the architect.
- Book II was the history of building developments, from the primitive mud huts to contemporary building materials. It included sun-dried and kiln-dried brick, Pozzolana, marble, tufa (a soft volcanic rock), and sandstone building blocks.
- Books III and IV covered site development, design, and decoration of temples, including the Doric, Ionic, and Corinthian orders.
- Book V described public buildings and facilities, such as forums, basilica, and baths.
- Book VI reported on the relationship between climate and building design.
- Book VII was about internal and external decoration, stucco, and coloring materials.
- Books VIII, IX, and X were mainly on water supply, astronomy, optics, and mechanical devices. These devices included cranes, water pumps, water wheels, catapults, and other siege engines. Vitruvius described how to arm *ballistas,* catapults, and *scorpions* by tuning them to a proper musical key. He also told how to design the frames, twisted sinew, and windlasses of battle engines. (Morgan; Knowland and Howe; Granger)

Archimedes

Herod's engineers were also familiar with the writings of the great scholar *Archimedes of Syracuse,* a Greek mathematician who combined mathematics, mechanics, and hydrostatics. In his *Principle of Archimedes,* he wrote the basic laws of ship design:

- The upward thrust on a body immersed in a fluid equals the weight of the fluid displaced by the body.
- The three natural states of a body in water are: a body whose density is equal to, less than, and greater than that of a liquid in which it is immersed.
- A body less dense than the liquid would float, and the portion of it which is submerged has the same ratio to the whole volume of the body as its whole weight had to that of an equal volume of water.
- If the body is forcibly held below the surface, it will exert an upward force equal to the difference between its own weight and the liquid it displaced. (Landels)

Archimedes' principles remain the basis of ship design to the present day.

Thales

Herod's engineers were also acquainted with the works of *Thales of Miletus.* Thales was an Ionic philosopher of the sixth century BCE. He was a military advisor and wrote about the natural science of the universe and practical techniques for measuring angles.

Hero

For machine design, Herod's engineers looked to *Hero,* who lived in the first century BCE and studied the theories of Archimedes. He was also a student of early technical writers *Strato of Lampsacus* and *Ctesibius.*

Hero's Mechanics, a complete treatise on the theory and application of practical mechanics, served as an engineering manual. It described the five elementary machines: windlass, lever, pulley, wedge, and worn gear. It also explained the *gear-ratio* and its implications, the *parallelogram of forces,* and the block and tackle arrangements.

Another of Hero's works was *Pneumatica,* which discussed

the properties of air, behavior of liquids, and the impossibility of a continuous vacuum. It explained why a liquid flows through a siphon.

Hero's books on *Metrica* dealt with pure geometry, plane figures, triangles, and segments of circles. He explained surveying and the use of instruments, sightings, and water levels for alignment. On the basis of Hero's books, surveyors used vertical poles with movable marker discs to find relative heights at various points of the ground.

Hero's writings involved both mechanics and warfare. These became the bases of investigation in the *School of Alexandria*. Topics included *geodesy,* the science of measurement of the earth's surface, *automata,* the science of moving machines, and *baroulcus,* methods of lifting heavy weights. Also included were the sciences of weights and measures, metrology, measuring instruments, lenses, mirrors, pneumatics, and waterpower.

The titles of Hero's books were as follows:

- *Pneumatica,* on air and liquids
- *Automatopoietike,* on automatic devices
- *Mechanica,* on machinery
- *Catoptrica,* on mirrors
- *Metrica,* on pure geometry
- *Dioptra,* on surveying
- *Geometrica, Sereometrica,* on solid geometry
- *Belopoeca,* on catapult construction
- *Cheiroballistra,* on hand catapults

Pliny

Another great thinker of the time was *Pliny,* born in 23 CE. His full name was *Gaius Plinius Secundus,* but he was better known as *Pliny the Elder* to distinguish him from his nephew. In 69 CE he became the Chief of the Fleet under Emperor Vespasian.

Although Pliny wrote his treatises soon after the end of the Herodian Period, his works showed the state of mathematics and science of the time.

Pliny's magnus opus was *Naturalis Historia,* consisting of 37 books in which he listed more than 20,000 important facts.

- Book 1 was an index of topics and sources.
- Book 2 covered the universe, stars, planets, and astronomy.

- Book 3 to 6 were descriptions of world geography.
- Books 7 to 11 covered human and animal anatomy.
- Books 12 to 32 were on botany and medical substances.
- Books 33 to 37 described mineral substances, including metals, stones, mining, metallurgy, and the use of these materials in medicine, painting, and architecture (Landels).

Numerals

Though Mesopotamian scribes used a "sexagesimal" system for calculating numbers (i.e., base-60; see below under Mathematics), their system for writing numbers was partially decimal. They used cuneiform wedges as numerals. Figure 4-1 shows some of these ancient characters and numerals. A short, vertical wedge "V" would represent units of 1, while a short, horizontal wedge ">" would represent a unit of 10 as shown on page 58:

Figure 4-1
Mathematics and numerals

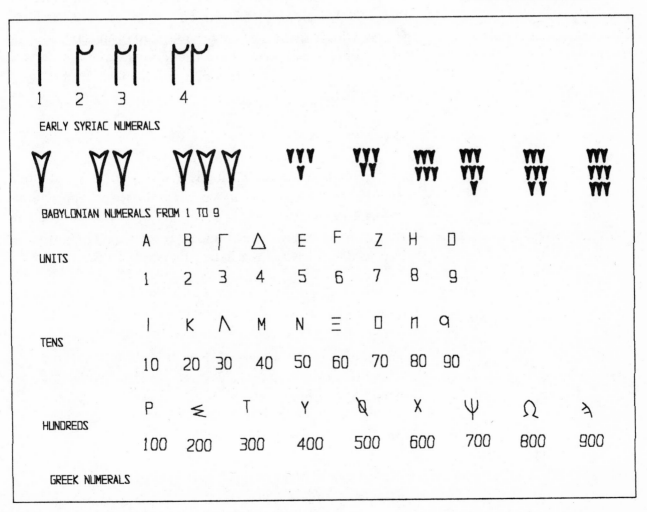

$$V \qquad = 1$$

$$>VVV \qquad = 13$$

$$>>V \qquad = 21$$

$$\begin{array}{l} VVV \\ >>VV \qquad = 25 \end{array}$$

$$\begin{array}{l} VVV \\ VVV \\ >>>VVV = 39 \end{array}$$

Early Hebrew inscriptions contained symbols that indicated numbers, although it was more common during the Maccabeean Period for numbers to be represented by letters of the alphabet. Letters *aleph* to *tet* stood for single digit units in succession: 1, 2, 3, 4, 5, 6, 7, 8, and 9. *Yod* to *tzadi* were used for tens: 10, 20, 30, 40, 50, 60, 70, 80, and 90. *Qof* to *tav* represented hundreds up to 400. In the Talmud, combinations of letters formed numbers above 400. For example, 500 was written *tav-qof* (400 + 100), 900 was written *tav-tav-qof* (400 + 400 + 100), and so forth.

The Romans used a system of letters to represent certain quantities. First, they used the following numbers to represent specific values:

I = 1, V = 5, X = 10, L = 50, C = 100, D = 500, M = 1000

They would then use combinations of these letters for all other quantities. In these combinations, when the letter representing the smaller value was placed to the right, it was to be added to the value represented by the previous letter. Conversely, when it was placed to the left, it was to be subtracted. Thus:

VI = 6, XI = 11
IV = 4, IX = 9

Sometimes a combination could have both:

MMCDLIX = 2459

Where:

MM = 1000 + 1000
CD = 500 – 100 = 400

L = 50

IX = 10 − 1 = 9

A bar drawn over the letters meant that the quantity was to be multiplied by 1000:

$$\overline{XIII} = 13,000$$

Mathematics

The early Sumerians used clay tablets for record keeping. They pressed a rounded or pointed stick on the surface of wet clay tablets, forming circular, semicircular, or wedge-shaped characters. The blocks were then baked by fire or dried in the sun.

Early Babylonian and Greek mathematics were used to measure land and quantities of material. Symbols and numerals were inscribed on cuneiform tablets for multiplication tables, reciprocals, and square roots.

Unlike the base-10 mathematical system that we use today, the ancient Mesopotamians used a base-60, or "sexagesimal," system for all calculations. Remnants of this system still exist today in units of time, whereby hours and minutes are divided into units of sixty, and circles are divided into 360 degrees.

Throughout the ancient world, including Greece and Mesopotamia, there was a highly developed tradition of exact sciences. This included mathematics, astronomy, and related fields. One well-known work from this tradition was Euclid's *Elements,* written in 3000 BCE. This was a treatise on geometry, proportions, and the theory of numbers. One piece of knowledge preserved from that work is the *Pythagorean Theorem*:

> The square of the hypotenuse of a right triangle is equal to the sum of the squares of the sides.

On the basis of this theorem, which was also known in some form in Mesopotamia, ancient engineers knew that a triangle with sides of three, four, and five cubits would form a right triangle. They used this rule to lay out square or rectangular buildings, as shown in Figure 4-2.

As early as 3100 BCE, merchants in Mesopotamia developed cuneiform script on clay tablets as an early form of bookkeeping. For quick calculations that did not require preserving

"a" may be any corner of the building.
"ab" may be taken along any side of the building.
Strike a 40 c radius from "a"
Strike a 50 c radius from "e"
Point of intersection is on 90 degree line to "ab"
Note: c = Cubit

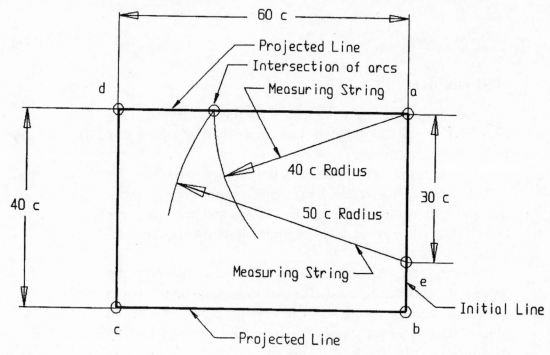

Figure 4-2
Squaring building lines with a
measuring string

records, merchants used wax tablets to add, subtract, and multiply. To aid them in calculations, ancient scribes would often compile lists of common calculations such as squares and cubes of numbers. We have ancient lists of numbers from 1 to 60 squared and from 1 to 32 cubed. For multiplication, the Egyptians, Greeks, Romans, and Judeans commonly used the abacus, shown in Figure 4-3.

By means of lines and rectangles, mathematicians could prove formulas without using algebraic shorthand. As example, they could prove the *Quadratic Equation*

$$(a + b)^2 = a^2 + 2ab + b^2$$

by drawing a set of rectangles, as shown in Figure 4-4.

An important branch of mathematics required by Herod's surveyors and builders was *geometry.* This term comes from the Greek words for "earth" and "to measure." Figure 4-5 is a dia-

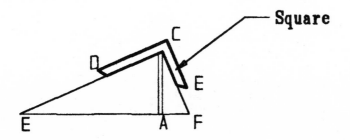

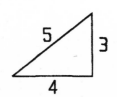

The Quadratum Geometricum   **3-4-5 Right Triangle**

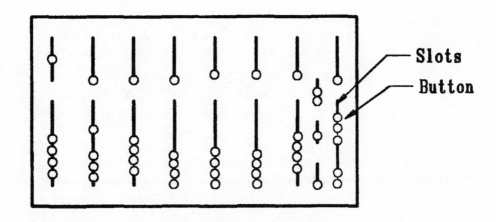

Roman Abacus

Figure 4-3
Calculating devices

gram showing how *Eratosthenes* estimated the earth's diameter by employing mathematical theories, geometrical methods, and the course of the sun. He found that the sun at noonday was exactly in the zenith at Syene (First Cataract of the Nile) when it was 7 degrees 12 minutes south of the zenith at Alexandria. Since the distance between the two points was 5,000 stadia, he calculated that the earth's diameter was 7,850 miles. This was only 50 miles less than the polar diameter, as we know it.

Ancient Egyptians also used geometry to resurvey the boundaries of their farms after the yearly floods of the Nile River. This process of resurveying is mentioned by Herodotus, a Greek writer of the fifth century BCE, when he discusses the Egyptian King Sesostris:

The king divided the land among all Egyptians so that to each he gave a quadrangle of equal size. (DeCamp; Schwartz)

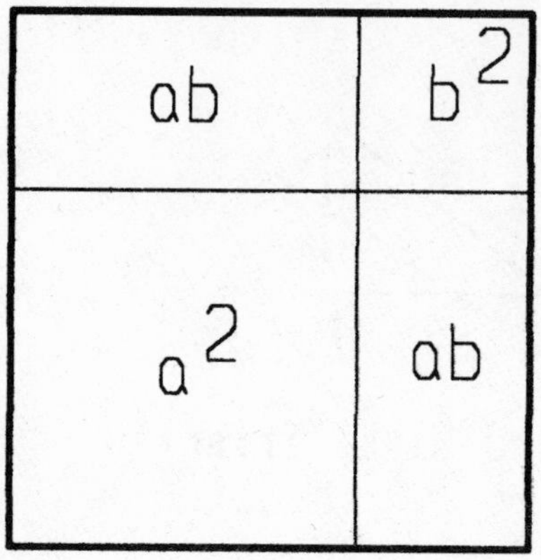

$$(a+b)^2 = a^2 + 2ab + b^2$$

$$(a+b)(a-b) = a^2 - b^2$$

Figure 4-4
Quadratic equation

The art of surveying, then, was well advanced before the building of the Temple Mount. Engineers knew how to find the properties and dimensions of circles, cubes, cylinders, ellipses, hexagon, and spheres. Military engineers used this technology in the design and operation of catapults. See the section on Surveying later in this chapter.

Writing Materials

During the biblical period the three most common types of writing material were papyrus, leather, and ostraca. The Egyptians, Greeks, and Romans most commonly used papyrus. They used it in preparing manuscripts and commercial documents, from the fourth century BCE to the fourth century CE. See Figure 4-6. Papyrus sheets were made from the pith of papyrus plants that had been sliced into longitudinal strips. After laying these strips side by side into rectangular units, they superimposed another mat with the strips running at right angles to it. They added water (and perhaps glue) and then applied pressure, converting the layers into a homogeneous mass, which they dried, polished, and made ready for use.

The papyrus plant was not native to Judea, and therefore it needed to be imported from such places as Egypt. Because of this added expense, papyrus was not as commonly used in Judea. Leather made from animal skins was more commonly used as a writing material during biblical times.

Because of the expense of producing papyrus and leather, broken shards of pottery, or *ostraca* (singular: *ostracon*), were used as an inexpensive substitute. Ostraca were used for simple needs such as receipts, ration lists, and even letters.

Ink in biblical times was a solution of charcoal, or soot, and di-

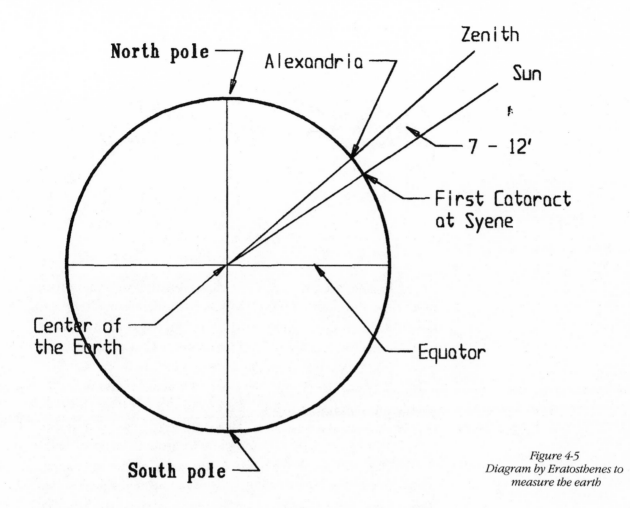

Figure 4-5
Diagram by Eratosthenes to
measure the earth

luted gum. Scribes used an inkhorn with a small hollow recepta-cle for ink. They carried this, along with reed pens, in an oblong case that was usually worn like a dagger thrust behind the scribe's girdle.

It was customary to write treatises on long sheets of parch-ment or papyrus. Separate parts of a manuscript were rolled up and called volumes (the English word being derived from the Latin *volvere* "to roll"). For longer works, several sheets could be sewn together to form a longer writing surface. When the rolls became too large, they were cut into smaller rolls, or *biblia*, meaning "books" in Greek. Thus, longer works from antiquity are normally divided into "books"; Josephus' *Jewish Antiquities*, for example, is divided into 20 books.

Measurement of Lengths

Most ancient cultures used parts of the body as units of measure-ment. More accurate lengths became important when man began

Figure 4-6
A scribe

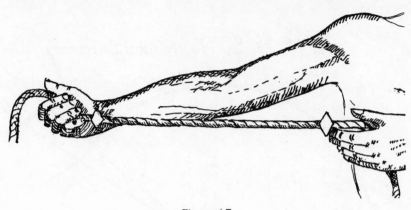

Figure 4-7
One cubit between buttons

to divide land. As long as rough measurements were adequate, then the breadth of the palm, lengths of the forearm, distance of the stride, and height were satisfactory, but these units of measurement had to be standardized for accuracy. Consequently, royal cubits (see below) were made into standard units by Egyptian, Sumerian, Assyrian, Greek, Persian, and Roman rulers.

Still, ancient systems of measurement did not have the same degree of precision as their modern counterparts. Furthermore, because the Bible was not necessarily meant to be a technical manual for professional engineers and architects, it would not necessarily use exact, precise figures when giving measurements. Therefore, we can only approximate when translating biblical units of measurement into modern equivalents (and furthermore, "biblical" units of measurement were often slightly different in the Christian New Testament). In addition, these units of measurement could differ from region to region. With that in mind, let us consider the main units of measure used in the Bible:

Figure 4-8
*A rough way of measuring
distances by cubits*

- The most common unit of length was the *cubit,* which was the distance from the tip of the middle finger to the elbow, normally 17 to 21 inches. The length varied with the ruler at the time and place. Figures 4-7 and 4-8 show how a cubit is measured with a measuring rope.
- Units smaller than the cubit included the *span,* the *handbreadth* (or palm), and the *finger.*
- A *span* was the distance from the tip of the middle finger to the tip of the thumb with the fingers spread. Two spans equaled one cubit.
- Three *handbreaths* equaled one span.
- Four *fingers* equaled one handbreadth. See Figure 4-9.

Scholars do not agree on how to convert these units into modern units of measurements, or even whether it is possible to do so. Conventionally, a cubit is regarded as roughly 18 inches or 50 cm.

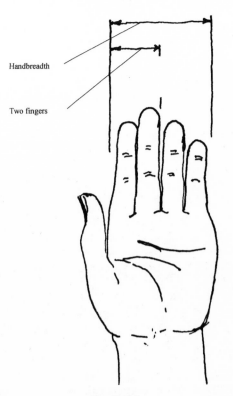

- *A fathom* was equivalent to a man's height, also equal to 72 inches, four cubits, or the distance between fingertips with arms outstretched.
- A *range* was the distance that a bow could shoot an arrow (Gen 21:16).
- A *short distance* was a two-hour *journey* (Gen 35:16, 48:7, 2 Kings 5:19).
- A *long distance* was a three-day's journey or more (Gen 30:36, 31:23).
- A *mile,* as used by the Persians, was 1,000 fathoms. The word *mile* came from the Latin words *mille passuum,* which meant *a thousand paces.*
- The Roman *pace* consisted of two steps (about five feet).
- One *land mile* was equal to 1,000 paces, 5,280 feet, 8 *stadia,* or 1,665 yards
- *One mile was equal to 1,000 units or 1,000 double steps, or 8 stadia*
- *One foot was equal to 295.7 mm or 13 1/2 digits*

Figure 4-9
Handbreadth

Josephus also described Jewish measures as follows:

• Standard cubit:	1 cubit	21 inches
• Zereth, or large span:	1/2 cubit	10.5 inches
• Small span:	1/3 cubit	7 inches
• Palm, or handbreath:	1/6 cubit	3.5 inches
• Inch, or thumb breadth:	1/18 cubit	1.16 inches
• Digit, or finger width:	1/24 cubit	.875 inch
• Fathom:	4 cubits	84 inches
• Schoenus, or line:	80 cubits	140 feet
• Jewish mile:	4,000 cubits	7,000 feet
• Stadium, or furlong:	400 cubits	700 feet

Josephus described measurements of dry volumes as follows:

- Bushel: about a peck
- Cab, or kab: about two quarts
- Ephah: three seah, and in liquid, to a bath, containing about a bushel and a half
- Half-homer: about five and a half bushels
- Homer: about eleven bushels, a cor or ten ephah

- Omer: about one bushel
- Seah: about a peck and a half
- Tenth deal: about a gallon, one-tenth of an ephah

Measurements of liquid volumes were given as follows:

- Bath: about eight gallons and a half
- Firkin: nearly nine gallons
- Hin: about a gallon and a half
- Log: about a pint, one-twelfth of a hin

Some Old Testament weights were given as follows:

- Talent (60 Minas):   75.558 grams
- Mina (50 shekels):   20.148 ounces
- Shekel (2 Bekas):   176.29 grains
- Beka (10 Geras):   88.14 grains
- Gerath: 8.81 grains

Vitruvius recognized the importance of devices used for standardizing and measuring weights in the following:

> The discovery of the method of testing weights by steel yards and balances saves us from fraud, by introducing honest practices into life. (Whiston)

As was noted before, most measurements given in the Bible are approximate. The size of Solomon's Temple in the book of Ezekiel is an example. The smallest measurement is one cubit and the largest is 500 cubits. Lengths are given as 1, 1½, 2, 3, 5, 6, 10, 25, 50, 70, 100, and 500 cubits. Errors in long measurements could be plus or minus 100 cubits (155 feet), and in small measurements errors could be plus or minus one cubit.

Surveying

In ancient Mesopotamia, clay tablets were used to record surveys, with areas divided into rectangles and triangles. These tablets contained measurements and statistics for specific property. Herod's surveyors measured distances with a high degree of accuracy, making both topographic and construction surveys for the design and building of the Temple Mount. These surveyors employed geometry and trigonometry and recorded the data on papyrus sheets. They set survey stakes in the field at the corners of the proposed structures.

Horizontal planes and right angles were made with an instrument known as the *libra, libella,* or *chorobate.* Other measuring devices mentioned in the Bible were the *measuring or flax line* (Amos 7:17, Zech. 2:5, Jer. 31:39) and the *measuring reed* (Ezek. 40:3).

Because property rights were as important in biblical times as they are now—if not more so—it was important that all property boundaries be properly surveyed and marked. In the ancient world, they were commonly marked with boundary stones. In order to preserve the sanctity of these property rights, the Bible legislated against any fraudulent disturbing of these boundary markers:

> Thou shalt not remove thy neighbor's landmark. (Deut. 19:14)
> Cursed be he that removeth his neighbor's landmark. (Deut. 27:17)

The setting of boundaries was important in any land transaction, even at the time of Abraham, as we can see in the biblical account of his acquisition of the Machpelah in Hebron:

> And Abraham harkened onto Ephron; and Abraham weighed to Ephron the silver, which he had named in the hearing of the children of Heth, four hundred shekels of silver: current money with the merchant. So the field of Ephron, which was in Machpelah, which was before Mamre, the field, and the cave which was therein, and all the trees that were in the field, that were in all the borders thereof round about, were made sure unto Abraham for a possession in the presence of the children of Heth, before all that went in at the gate of his city. (Gen. 23:16-18)

Building Codes

Building codes were not unknown in the legal traditions of the ancient world. Perhaps the most famous legal code from the ancient world is that of King Hammurabi of Babylon (1750–1700 BCE), who had his laws—almost 300 of them—inscribed on a seven-foot-high stone *stele.* A stele was an upright stone slab that served as a monument, marker, or memorial. Laws 229–233 regulate damages resulting from building construction:

- If a builder builds a house for a man and does not make its construction firm and the house which he built collapses and causes the death of the owner of the house—that builder shall be put to death.
- If it causes the death of the son of the owner of the house—they should put to death the son of the builder.
- If it causes the death of a slave of the owner of the house—he shall give to the owner of the house a slave of equal value.
- If it destroys property, he shall restore whatever it destroyed, and because he did not make the house which he built firm and it collapsed, he shall rebuild the house which collapsed at his own expense.
- If a builder builds a house for a man and does not make its construction meet the requirements and a wall fall in, the builder shall strengthen the wall at his own expense. (De Camp; Schwartz; J. Miller)

Constructing and maintaining irrigation canals was vital in ancient Mesopotamia, and Hammurabi's laws reflected this reality, as in Law 55:

The gentleman who opens his wall for irrigation purposes, but did not make his dike strong enough and hence caused a flood and inundated a field adjoining his, shall give grain to the owner of the field on the basis of those adjoining. (De Camp; Schwartz; J. Miller)

A letter Hammurabi wrote to his governors about the repair of canals exemplifies the importance of maintenance:

Unto Governor Sid-Iddinam say: Thus saith Hammurabi. Thou shalt call out the men who hold lands along banks of the Damanum-Canal that they may clear out Damamum-Canal. Within the present month shall they complete the work. (De Camp; Schwartz; J. Miller)

The early Greeks did not have an actual building code, but rather some complicated sets of specifications governing the contractual relationship. According to fragments found in the restoration of a building built in 341 BCE, the completion date, the names of contractor and the inspector of construction were engraved on the stone. Qualities of workmanship and the methods of inspection of a masonry project were described as follows:

> He shall set the joints against each other, fitting, and before inserting dowels he shall show the architect all the stones [to be] fitting, and shall set them straight and sound and dowel them with iron dowels, two dowels to each stone of each course, and one to the stone at the corner. (Winter)

It would seem that these stones were to be laid with their long sides touching. The cornerstone of each course could then be doweled only on its short side and could receive only one dowel comfortably.

> The clause is a natural one, and has good parallel in the Lebadeia inscription: "He shall [perform] in person, in presence of the commissioners, the insertion of dowels and clamps and the pouring of lead, and shall close no [joint] without having shown it." (Winter)

According to an archaeologist who examined the tablets, the inscription meant:

> . . . having made the margins of the joints as the architect shall order; "and before leading the stones he shall show the architect the top surfaces and all the joints, and shall dowel with iron dowels. . . ." This is the only procedure which will ensure accurate supervision of the preparation of contact surfaces. (Winter)

The Bible also contains building regulations. Because the typical roof was flat, and during the hot summer months residents would sleep on the breezy rooftops, it was necessary to take measures to prevent people from falling off roofs:

> When thou buildest a new house, then thou shalt make a parapet for thy roof, that thou bring not blood upon thy house, if any man fall from thence. (Deut. 22:8)

The Bible mandated roof-edge protection because the ancient Hebrews used rooftops not only for sleeping, but for preparing food and doing other household chores. This regulation carried over to the modern building and safety codes.

Summary

In summary, biblical history was concurrent with the work of early mathematicians and scientists, as shown in the following chart:

1700 BCE	Hammurabi invokes building laws
1650	Ahmes, an Egyptian scribe, writes a book on mathematics
600	Thales demonstrates geometry
540	Pythagorus describes geometry and the theory of numbers
460	Hippocrates of Chios writes on geometry
450	Herodotus, historian
404	Plato establishes foundation of mathematics
340	Aristotle, application of mathematics, logic
336	Alexander the Great establishes the Macedonian Empire
335	Eudemus
334	Alexander in Asia
320	Decarchies
300	Euclid, geometry
287	Gauls invade Macedonia and Greece
270	Strato of Lampsacus
225	Archimedes, geometry, mechanics
146	Greece and Macedonia become part of the Roman Empire
140	Hipparchus writes on astronomy and trigonometry. Hero and Ptolmy write on astronomy, geography, and optics
75	Cicero
30	Vitruvius, Frontinus
10 CE	Strabo, history of mathematics
50	Heron of Alexandria, geodesy, mathematics; Pliny; Plutarch; Aristaeus

CHAPTER 5

Construction Materials

In biblical times the most important building material was stone. Its strength, durability, and pleasing appearance made it the preferred material in the construction of royal buildings.

Wood was also an important construction material. Ancient engineers built wood-framed roofs with heavy cedar timbers, covered with wood planks. They made gates and doors of elaborately carved wood hung from bronze hinges. Figures 5-1 and 5-2 show how they cut and dressed logs to turn them into lumber.

The Temple Mount project required immense quantities of building materials, which builders located, transported, and prepared for installation on a mountaintop. Fortunately, the Holy Land and nearby Lebanon were blessed with most of the needed resources.

Quarrying Limestone

One hundred million years ago, Jerusalem lay at the sea bottom. Over eons, the skeletons and shells of microscopic sea animals were deposited, forming thick beds. These were consolidated under heavy layers of sediment to form limestone. Slowly, tectonic action of the earth's crust thrust these formations upward, creating limestone mountains, and these mountains served King Solomon and Herod the Great as vast quarries from which they extracted, dressed, and transported limestone blocks to build their great temples.

Quarrying operations in biblical times were similar to those of the present day. They involved the following tasks:

- Removing the overburden of soil and inferior stone
- Cutting the loosening large blocks of stone with pegs, as shown in Figure 5-3

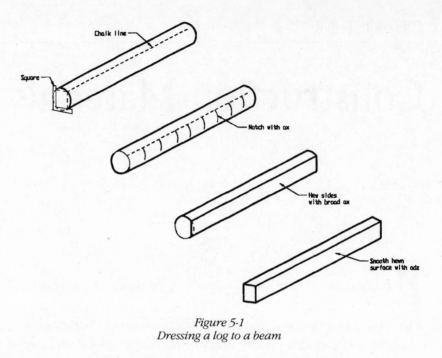

Figure 5-1
Dressing a log to a beam

- Dressing stone blocks into finished shapes, as shown in Figure 5-4

Where limestone beds were about 10 feet deep, quarrymen cut long grooves into the top of the beds. Then they drove wooden wedges into the grooves and soaked them with water, so that the wood would swell. The swollen wedges then split the rock along the groove line. Finally, the workers loosened the stone blocks by wedging and undercutting.

Where limestone was in thinner layers, the quarrymen drilled a row of holes along a line to be fractured. They drove wooden pegs into the holes and soaked them with water. When the pegs expanded, they split the limestone along a rough line. Workers then lifted the thin layers from the horizontal joints.

Stonecutters shaped the rough faces of the stone block with saws, chisels, and adzes. They dressed horizontal and vertical surfaces using squares, plumb bobs, levels, and measuring strings. Then they finished the blocks to a smooth surface with rubbing stones. The use of limestone as building blocks is reflected in the biblical account of the construction of Solomon's Temple.

And the king commanded, and they quarried great stones, costly stones, to lay the foundation of the house with hewn stones. (1 Kings 5:31)

Figure 5-2
Dressing logs to beams

For columns and facing, they preferred marble, a metamorphic rock that could be carved and polished. Most marble came from the Aegean Islands, Greece, and Rome. Granite, an igneous rock produced by heat and pressure deep in the earth's crust, was found to be more durable than limestone or marble, but it was difficult to cut and finish. Because of its greater strength, granite blocks were used for foundations.

Herod's quarrymen surveyed the local limestone deposits to select the best quarry location based on the following criteria:

Figure 5-3
Quarrymen splitting stone
blocks with pegs

- Will the stones cut from this location be large enough for their purpose?
- Will the type of limestone weather well?
- Can the stone be effectively cut and carved?

Several sites fit these criteria. Layer thickness determined the final use of the stone. They used thin layers for pavers and thicker layers for building blocks.

Herod's stonecutters worked in teams of five or six. Each man cut a 4-inch wide groove until he reached the required depth. He used a two-handed pick and worked downward. The height of the course determined the distance between men. When the cuts reached the required depth, they cut the blocks by working in from the ends.

Figure 5-4
Dressing stone blocks

In the quarry they used picks, crowbars, drills, hammers, wedges, plugs, and feathers (iron wedges). For channeling, they used picks with a narrow wedge. They used crowbars to separate layers of stone, and they set wedge-shaped iron feathers into the opening. Then they placed iron plugs between feathers and drove them in with a heavy maul. The great force thus exerted on the sides of the channel separated the blocks of stone. They then cut holes for the plugs with bow-drills.

After the quarrymen cut and removed a stone block from the rock formation, they dressed the block in various finishes, using hard stone balls, like *diorite,* to pound the soft limestone surface. One man could grind down a square foot of surface one inch in a five-hour shift.

Stone blocks were classified according to their finish:

- *Unsquared stones* were rough-cut pieces as they came from the quarry. These were used mainly for backing in a masonry structure and were not exposed.
- *Squared stones* were quarry-faced, pitched-face, or drafted

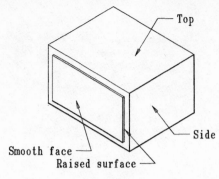

Figure 5-5
Herodian smooth block

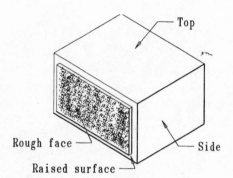

Figure 5-6
Herodian rough block

Figure 5-7
Rubble wall

stones. The surfaces were rough-pointed, bush-hammered, rubbed, honed, or polished, as shown in Figures 5-5 and 5-6.

The cut stones were classified according to their shape and use:

- *Building stones* were hewn to regular shapes.
- *Split stones,* also called *flagstones* or *flagging,* were one-half to two inches thick and were used for pavements.
- *Cobbles* were large pieces of irregular shape and were used for massive construction.
- *Crushed stones* were used for backfilling of walls.

Stone Masonry

Masonry work was classified by finish, patterns, and type of horizontal joints:

- *Rubble* had broken joints set in random patterns and was laid without mortar, as shown in Figure 5-7.
- *Dressed rubble* had dressed joints set in random patterns and fitted close together.
- *Broken coursed ashlars* had different size square stones in the same wall. See Figure 5-8.
- *Regular coursed ashlars* had regular, uniform courses, similar to brickwork. See Figure 5-9.
- *Ranged masonry* had all courses of the same thickness.
- *Broken range masonry* had some courses of uniform thickness.
- *Random coursed masonry* had no uniform courses.

Workers would transport the rough stone blocks from the quarry in a variety of ways. In the chord method, they would cut a block from the quarry face, then cut and dress it into a cylindrical shape. Then they rolled the cylinder from the quarry to the site and cut one chord. They rotated the block in place to rest on the chord face and cut the other three chords. By this method, they changed a cube-shaped block to a cylinder, then back again into a smaller block. In another method, they shaped the stone into a drum, then rolled it to the building site.

According to 1 Kings 6:7, the stone quarried for Solomon's Temple was dressed at the quarry, but this was probably an exceptional case. Quarrymen usually dressed large masonry blocks at the building site rather than at the quarry. Stone dressing operation required about 120 hours per cubic meter of stone block; 200 workers could produce about eight cubic meters of stone block per working day.

After the blocks were dressed, they were moved to a storage and loading area. At the storage area, the men hoisted each block with an A-frame crane and transported it by an ox-driven two-wheel cart. They brought larger stone blocks, weighing 50 to 60 tons, as close as possible to the construction site. These were transported over wooden rollers and pulled by oxen or manpower to their final location. Thirty workers took one full day to move a 50-ton block using three cranes.

Although rubble masonry walls appeared to be randomly placed, they were in fact methodically positioned. The weight of each stone was set straight down on the one beneath it. Mislaid stones could slide out. Stonemasons shaped the blocks with a hammer and chisel and then used small stone pieces as shims. Small blocks required mortar, and large stones relied on friction.

A typical cornerstone in the Temple Mount retaining wall weighed about 50 tons. One of the largest ashlar stones used in the Western Wall was over 40 feet long, 11 feet high, and 14 feet thick. This immense stone weighed over 517 tons[1] and was flanked by two other large stones, one 18 feet long and the other 9.3 feet long (Bahat).

Another large stone in the edifice, placed in the twenty-eighth layer of the south wall at the threshold of the gate, was 24 feet long and 6 feet high and weighed over 100 tons (*Encyclopedia Judaica* 15:963). Other huge stone blocks were set in the southwest corner of the Temple Mount. One was 33 feet by 7 feet by 3 feet. The bottom of the west wall was about 50 feet thick and built three blocks wide.

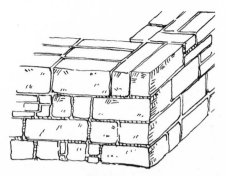

Figure 5-8
Wall of broken coursed ashlars

Figure 5-9
Laying up a wall of uniform coursed ashlars

Columns

The workers cut, dressed, and installed the stone columns in the porticos as supports for the lintels. Stonemasons used various methods for cutting and finishing stone columns.

In one method, they first reduced the stone to a *parallelopiped,* which is a six-faced solid. Then they made a wooden tem-

[1] The stone was 42 x 11 x 14, by 160/2000, resulting in a volume of 6,468 cubic feet. Since limestone weighs about 160 pounds per cubic foot, the block would weigh 1,034,880 pounds, or 517 tons.

plate, shaped like an arc, of the same radius as the finished column. They chipped and ground down the surface of the stone to conform to the template.

In another method, the stonemasons cut each end of the column to the required shape and pulled a stringline between the ends to control the shaping of the balance of the column. Column capitals were made separately. They were sculpted into four principal designs: Doric, Ionic, Corinthian, and Composite.

Herod's stonemasons appear to have quarried these columns in the Jerusalem area; the remains of some unfinished columns have been discovered there. These apparently were left unfinished because the stone had cracked in the process of quarrying. One such unfinished column found in the Mahaneh Yehudah quarter of Jerusalem measures about 23 feet high (*Encyclopedia Judaica* 15:966).

Solid one-piece columns were very heavy. A two-foot diameter by ten-foot long column weighed about 4,700 pounds. A three-foot diameter column of the same length weighed about 10,200 pounds.

Timber

Herod's millwrights and carpenters used cedar, fir, or pine timber for framing the Temple and portico roofs. Cedar trees, a type of conifer, grow on the Lebanese mountains at an elevation of more than 3,000 feet. Some trees grew over 50 feet tall, with straight trunks ideal for ships' masts or gin poles. According to the Bible, much of the timber used for the construction of the First Temple was acquired from Lebanon, since King Solomon traded with King Hiram of Tyre:

> So Hiram gave Solomon timber of cedar and timber of cypress according to all his desire. (1 Kings 5:24)
> Now Hiram the king of Tyre had furnished Solomon with cedar-trees and cypress-trees, and with gold, according to all his desire. . . . (1 Kings 9:11)

Vitruvius, the Roman engineer, described how to cure standing timber before felling. He recommended that the trunk be cut to the heart and allowed to bleed until dry. Only then should the tree be cut down. Also, trees should be felled in early autumn, not in spring. Green wood is heavier and more easily bruised.

Biblical carpenters learned many *tricks of the trade* from contemporary shipbuilders. They used similar framing skills and tools to build towers, cranes, and buildings. Shipbuilders knew that the ships' masts had to be straight and strong enough to withstand wind forces and that ships' keels and ribs had to resist water pressure. Herod's shipwrights taught carpenters how to fasten wood-framing members together. They interlocked timbers with mortise and tenon, iron connectors, nails, plates, and wood dowels. See Figure 5-10. The following are examples of timber connectors:

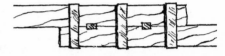

Figure 5-10
Timber connections with dowels

- Straight bolted splices
- Lapped splices with iron keys and bolts
- Butt joints with timber fish plate, keyed and bolted
- Butt joints with double timber fish plate, bolted
- Compression beam, bolted and held in place by fish plates and bolts
- Splicing by breaking joints and bolting
- Lap splices with hardwood keys and yoke straps
- Scarf-and-butt splices, with one fish plate bolted
- Lap-and-scarf butt joints, keyed with hardwood and locked with anchor fish plate and bolts
- Butt-and-lap plates and scarf joints
- Bending scarf joints

Herod's shipbuilders and carpenters used rulers, adjustable triangles, plumb bobs (plummets), dividers, compasses, calipers, and square sets to lay out their work.

Metals

Throughout the eastern Mediterranean, long before Herod's time, Alexander the Great was one of the first to wear an iron helmet (De Camp 116). Wrought iron rods were used to reinforce the marble ceiling beams in the *Propylaia,* the monumental gateway to the *Acropolis* in Greece.

Herod's builders used lead and iron in stone masonry. They interlocked stone ashlars and columns with metal dowels and anchors to resist wind, earthquakes, and ground settlement. Josephus described this system as follows:

. . . he laid rocks together and bound them one to another with lead, and included some of the inner parts till it proceeded to a great height, and till both largeness of the square edifice and its altitude were immense and till the vastness of the stones in the front were plainly visible from the outside, yet so the inward parts were fastened together with iron, and preserved the joints immovable for all future times. (Ant 15:398–99)

Fuels

During the Herodian Period, the people burned wood and charcoal for cooking and smithing. They preferred charcoal for cooking because it burned slower and made less smoke than wood. Blacksmiths used charcoal in their metal-smelting furnaces because it could reach very high temperatures. Generally, the blacksmiths were unable to get their furnaces above 1150 degrees Fahrenheit and so their ability for making steel was limited.

Charcoal making was an important activity in biblical times. It was produced by slow, partial combustion of wood. Oak and beech were the best woods for charcoal because they had the hardest and densest grain. Oak trees from Transjordan were cut into small sections and partially burned in pits. Then the pieces were further chopped into smaller particles and bagged for shipment.

Glass

During the Hellenistic Period, builders experimented with various translucent windowpane materials. They tried oiled cloth, sheepskin, mica, horn, and gypsum shaved down to a thin sheet. None was transparent. In the more affluent homes, these materials were replaced by glass, which had become clear enough for this purpose. In the later years of the Roman Period, glass was generally used to allow light into buildings through small round skylights.

Other Construction Materials

Herod's builders also used sand, lime, gypsum, Pozzolana, and clay for construction. They dug sand from selected pits and then washed it with water to remove the dirt and salt. Sand used for mortar and plaster consisted of irregular particles, not rounded beach sand.

Clay bricks were a common building material throughout the ancient world, especially in areas such as Mesopotamia, where quality stone and wood were not readily available. Chapter 5 of the book of Exodus gives a few details about the process of brick-making during biblical times. The Israelite slaves in Egypt probably would moisten the Nile Delta clay with water, add straw fibers, and then trample the mixture to a workable consistency. They would shape the dough-like material in wooden molds and, when the clay was partly dry, remove the bricks from the molds and stack them with airspace between to dry in the sun.

Baked brick, though long known, was not generally used until the late Roman Republic. Vitruvius wrote that mud brick was illegal for house walls within the city of Rome. Some builders baked clay into thin slabs to form tiles in many shapes and sizes. Romans preferred long, wide bricks, about 1½ inches thick. Such shapes were less likely to warp or crack than the thicker forms.

Gypsum

The name *gypsum* came from the ancient Greek word *gypsos,* meaning chalk. As early as 3000 BCE, it was used by the Egyptians to line the interiors of their pyramids. The Greeks and Romans also used gypsum plaster in their temples and houses.

Builders made gypsum from a lightweight gray-white rock called *hydrated calcium sulfate.* Its geological origins are unknown, but prehistoric seas formed the gypsum deposits. Workers roasted gypsum-bearing ore in pits to form clinkers. They then crushed the clinkers to a talc-like powder, now known as *Plaster of Paris.* With water and sand added to the gypsum powder, a paste was formed that could be bonded to a masonry surface. As the paste dried and *cured,* the material returned to its original rocklike hardness.

Mortar

Mortar is a mixture of lime, sand, ashes, and water. When dry, this material forms a waterproof coating. Herod's builders used lime mortar as a plaster and to bond masonry together. They applied this material as a finish coating over clay masonry walls, roof decks, reservoirs, and cisterns.

Vitruvius described how mortar should be made (in *Book Two* of the *Ten Books on Architecture*):

1. In walls of masonry the first question must be with regard to the sand, in order that it may be fit to mix into mortar and

have no dirt in it. The kinds of pit are these: black, grey, red, and carbuncular. Of these the best to be found is that which crackles when rubbed in the hand, while that which has much dirt in it will not be sharp enough. Again: throw some sand upon a white garment and then shake it out; if the garment is not soiled and no dirt sticks to it, the sand is suitable.

2. But if there are no sandpits from which it can be dug, then we must sift it out of riverbeds or from gravel or even from the sea beach. This kind, however, has these defects when used in masonry: it dries slowly; the wall cannot be built up without interruption but from time to time there must be pauses in the work; and such a wall cannot carry vaulting. Furthermore, when sea-sand is used in walls and they are coated with stucco, a salty efflorescence is given out which spoils the surface.

3. But pit sand used in masonry dries quickly, the stucco coating is permanent, and the walls will support vaulting. I am speaking of sand fresh from the sand pits. For if it lies unused too long after being taken out, it is disintegrated by exposure to sun, moon, or hoarfrost, and becomes earthy. So when mixed in masonry, it has no binding power on the rubble, which consequently settles and down comes the load which the walls can no longer support. Fresh pit sand, however, in spite of all its excellence in concrete structures, is not equally useful in stucco, the richness of which, when the lime and straw are mixed with such sand, will cause it to crack as it dries on account. But river sand, though useless in "signinum" on account of its thinness, becomes perfectly solid in stucco when thoroughly worked by means of polishing instruments. (Morgan, Vitruvius)

Lime

Ancient masons burned crushed limestone to produce *lime,* or *quicklime.* They used lime as a mixture in making plaster and glass and in smelting of metals. Vitruvius specified how to make lime, as follows:

1. Sand and its sources having been thus treated, next with regard to lime, we must be careful that it is burned from a stone which, whether soft or hard, is in any case white. Lime made from a close-grained stone of the harder sort will be good in structural parts; lime of porous stone, in stucco. After slaking

it, mix your mortar, if using pit sand, in proportions of three parts of sand to one of lime; if using river or sea-sand, mix two parts of sand with one of lime. These will be the right proportions for the composition of the mixture. Further, in using river or sea-sand, the addition of a third part composed of burnt brick, pounded up and sifted, will make your mortar of a better composition to use.

2. The reason why lime makes a solid structure on being combined with water and sand seems to be this: that rocks, like all other bodies, are composed of the four elements. Those which contain a larger proportion of air, are soft; of water, are tough from the moisture; of earth, hard; and of fire, more brittle. Therefore, if limestone, without being burned, is merely pounded up small and then mixed with sand and so put into the work, the mass does not solidify nor can it hold together. But if the stone is first thrown into a kiln, it loses its former property of solidity by exposure to the great heat of the fire, and so with its strength burnt out and exhausted it is left with its pores open and empty. Hence, the moisture and air in the body of the stone being burnt out and set free, and only a residuum of heat being left lying it, if the stone is then emersed in water, the moisture, before the water can feel the influence of the fire, makes its way into the open pores; then the stone begins to get hot, and finally, after it cools off, the heat is rejected from the body of the lime.

3. Consequently, limestone when taken out of the kiln cannot be as heavy as when it was thrown in, but on being weighed, though its bulk remains the same as before, it is found to have lost about a third of its weight owing to the boiling of the water. Therefore, its pores being thus opened and its texture rendered loose, it readily mixes with sand, and hence the two materials cohere as they dry, unite with the rubble, and make a solid structure.

Summary

Herod's engineers and craftsmen were able to produce most of the construction tools and materials needed for building the Temple Mount. They had the technical resources and knowledge of many preceding civilizations as well as those of contemporary ones, such as Greece and Rome.

CHAPTER 6

Building the Temple Mount

The Temple Mount took its present shape under Herod the Great. He was an Idumaean Jew who managed to build a powerful political base in Judea and, through a combination of political guile and ruthlessness, established an infamous legacy that exists to this day.

Part of Herod's complicated political maneuvering was his attempt to maintain favor domestically among the Jewish political and religious establishment and at the same time reach out to other parts of the Roman Empire. As part of his domestic strategy, Herod married Mariamne, a member of the Hasmonean family, and the second of his ten wives, in the hopes of gaining legitimacy for his throne. Because of his great paranoia, however, he began to see members of his own family as potential rivals and eventually put many of them to death.

Because of Herod's desire to integrate Judea culturally into other parts of the Roman world, there were many non-Jews in his court, although Jews were in the majority. Many Greeks lived in Judea, and consequently, the Hellenistic culture mixed with the Jewish culture. Some of Herod's advisors and closest friends were Hellenists, as were his children's tutors.

These political maneuverings also influenced his building projects, especially his decision to devote such enormous resources to renovations of the Temple Mount. Herod hoped to curry favor with the Jewish religious establishment by putting the centerpiece of the Jewish world, the Jerusalem Temple, on a par with the other great architectural achievements of his time.

On the other hand, to curry favor with other parts of the Roman Empire, he patronized non-Jewish cultural projects as well. Herod's building program spread from Western Greece to Syria and the Levant. His building projects were an important asset to Emperor Augustus' policy of expanding the Roman Empire. Herod, trying to be as Roman as possible, became an important representative in the Eastern Mediterranean. His grandiose building plan was a tool by which the Roman revolution spread to the Levant and the Holy Land.

Herod was inspired more by Roman architecture than by its Greek counterpart. As a new Roman citizen, he became more attuned to Rome's ascent than to the decay of the Hellenistic world. Visiting Rome in 40 BCE, Herod found the city in the midst of a major architectural program and digested its techniques, which were unknown outside of Italy.

Herod's kingdom included Judea, Galilee, and Phoenicia. His major construction projects there were outlets for his natural energy. They included the fortress at *Herodium,* the fortress at *Macherus,* and the harbor at *Caesarea,* which became the main port and headquarters for the Romans in Judea.

Harbor at Caesarea

The harbor at Caesarea consisted of major breakwaters, docks, and warehouses, part of which are shown in Chapter 3 (Figure 3-11). The port was previously known as *Strato's Tower,* named after a Phoenician king, but Herod renamed it *Caesarea* to honor the Roman emperor.

Since Caesarea had no natural harbor, Herod's engineers built a 200-foot-wide breakwater for docking and anchoring vessels. This protected the inner harbor from the ravages of waves and currents from the southwest. To the north, he constructed a semicircular seawall that enclosed a marina. The northern breakwater measured 250 yards, and the southern one 600 yards. Josephus described the building of the harbor as follows:

> After Herod had marked out the comparative dimension of the harbor . . . he had blocks of stone sunk into twenty fathoms of sea—most of which were fifty-feet long, nine deep and ten abroad, some being even larger. When this submarine foundation had risen to water level, he built above the surface a mole 200 feet wide; one hundred of these were built out into the sea to break the force of the waves, and, therefore, called the breakwater, while the remainder supported the stone wall that encircled the harbor.

The Temple Mount

The Temple Mount complex was by far the most important project of King Herod's reign. In 20 BCE, the king was at the peak of his power when he began to expand the Temple Mount. It took 58 years for his project to be finally completed, but Herod did not live to see it. He died in 4 BCE.

According to Josephus, when Herod decided to expand the Temple Mount, he announced the following to his subjects:

> That the enterprise that I now prepare to undertake is the most pious and beautiful of our time, I will now make clear. For this was the temple which our fathers built to the Most Great God after their return from Babylon, but it lacked sixty cubits in height, the amount by which the first temple, built by Solomon, exceeded it. And yet no one should condemn our fathers for neglecting their pious duty, for it was not their fault that this temple is smaller. Rather it was Cyrus and Darius, the sons of Hystaspes, who prescribed these dimensions for building. Since our fathers were subject to them, and their descendants after them to the Macedonians, they had no opportunity to restore this first archetype of piety to its former size. (Ant 15:384–86)

He then, as a good politician, praised the Roman Empire as follows:

> But since, by the will of God, I am now ruler and there continues to be a long period of peace and abundance of wealth and great revenues, and—what is of most importance—the Romans, who are, so to speak, the masters of the world are [my] loyal friends, I will try to remedy this oversight caused by the necessity and subjection of that earlier time, and by the act of piety make full return to God for the gift of this kingdom. (Ant 15:387)

His stonemasons worked eight years on preparation alone. They quarried and dressed ashlars and transported them to the building site before the actual construction of the project began. Herod wanted to be sensitive to Jewish laws regarding purity in the holy sanctuary, and so only priests did the actual work on the Temple. It took another three years before the temple was dedicated.

Herod planned to double the size of the existing Temple Mount and ordered construction of an immense paved platform, or *esplanade*. Its open area covered 30 acres and was 2,420 feet above sea level. It was in the shape of an irregular four-sided polygon and was retained by four massive stone walls—930 feet on the south, 1,620 on the west, 1,050 on the north, and 1,550 along the east side. Figure 6-1 shows the Temple Mount and its major buildings.

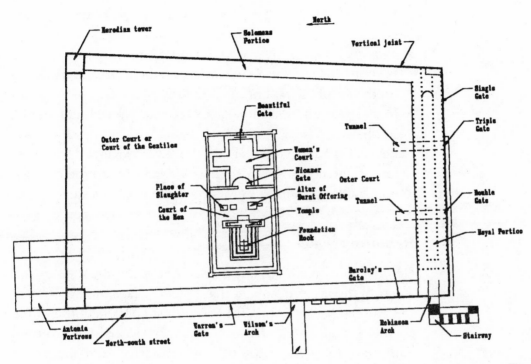

Figure 6-1
Plan of the Temple Mount

Herod declared that his objective was to exceed the beauty of the original Temple, which, according to Jewish tradition, was renowned for its great beauty and splendor:

Whoever did not see Jerusalem in the days of glory never saw a beautiful city in their life. (Babylonian Talmud Succah 51b)

Ten measures of beauty descended to the world, none were taken by Jerusalem. (Talmud Kiddushin 49b)

The First Temple Mount

Regarding the size of the original Temple Mount, the best available source of information is the book of Ezekiel, although one must be careful when using any information from this source, since his visions of the Temple (chapters 40–48) likely mixed idealized fantastic elements with actual historical data. According to Ezekiel 42:16–20, Solomon's Temple Mount was perfectly square and measured 500 by 500 cubits (about 750 by 750 feet). Similar measurements are given in the Mishnah (Middot 2:1).

Between the time of King Solomon and King Herod, the Temple Mount underwent several periods of construction and reconstruction:

- In about 970 BCE, King Solomon built the original square Mount.
- *Nebuchadnezzar* destroyed the First Temple in 586 BCE.
- In about 187 BCE, the Seleucids added the fortress *Akra* at the south wall of the Mount.
- In 141 BCE, the Hasmoneans expanded the Mount to the south.
- Between 19 and 11 BCE, Herod the Great expanded the structure to the north, south, and west. Expansion to the east was not practical, since the wall stood at the edge of a steep slope.

Retaining Walls

Herodian retaining walls enclosed all of the existing walls except a part of the Eastern Wall. At that time, the northerly portion of the Eastern Wall was original Solomonic construction and the southern part was Hasmonean. The two walls met at a vertical joint about 106 feet north of the southeastern corner of the present Temple Mount.

Different stone block finishes clearly show where the Hasmonean and Herodian walls met. Herodian ashlars have narrow regular borders with a smooth, slightly raised center, or *boss,* while Hasmonean blocks have irregular margins and a rough center. Figures 5-5 and 5-6 in Chapter 5 illustrate Herodian smooth and rough-faced blocks. Figure 6-2 shows a view of the Eastern Wall.

Surveying the Temple Mount Site

Herod's surveyors laid out the location of the new retaining walls using wooden poles, *dioptras,* leveling rods, and measuring cords. They employed the *royal cubit* and *fathom* for measuring distances and elevations. Figure 6-3 shows a typical transit.

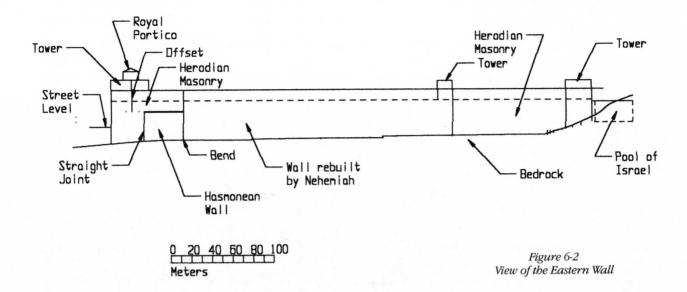

Figure 6-2
View of the Eastern Wall

The following describes how they may have laid out the perimeter of the Temple Mount.

- The surveyors set the southwest and southeast corners of the expanded Temple Mount at right angles to the Western Wall, as shown in Figure 6-4.
- Then they set the southeast corner at about 93 degrees and the northwest corner at 87 degrees. This formed the new outline of the Temple Mount.
- They placed long poles in the ground to mark the proposed corners, and set additional reference stakes around these points to ensure that their locations would not be lost.
- The engineers made the south and west lines the outside face of the new retaining walls, and the base lines for the balance of the project. They made all subsequent measurements perpendicular to these two base lines.
- Then they set wooden stakes over the entire construction area, forming a grid, or coordinate system. They inscribed on each stake its distance to the west or south base lines, as shown in Figure 6-5.
- For vertical measurements, the surveyors used the top of the Foundation Rock on Mount Moriah, located in the *Debir* of the Temple, as their main benchmark.
- They determined the ground elevation at each grid stake with *dioptras* and leveling rods.
- Scribes recorded this information on wax tablets, then prepared topographic maps on papyrus sheets. These data

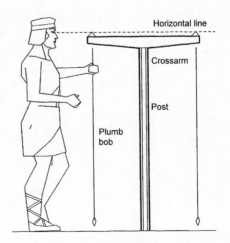

Figure 6-3
Biblical transit

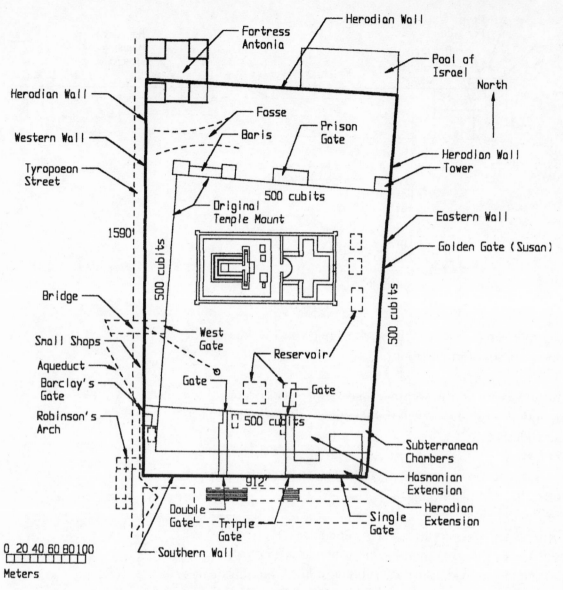

Figure 6-4
Condition of Temple Mount during times of Solomon and Herod

3. So Herod took away the old foundations, and laid others, and erected the Temple upon them, being in length a hundred cubits, and in height twenty additional cubits, which [twenty,] upon the sinking of their foundations, fell down: and this part it was that we resolved to raise again in the days of Nero. Now the Temple was built of stones that were white and strong, and each of their length was twenty-five cubits, their height was eight, and their breadth about twelve; and the whole structure, as also the structure of the royal cloister, was on each side much lower, but the middle was much higher, till they were visible to those that dwelt in the country for a great many furlongs, but chiefly to such as lived over against them and those that approached to them. The Temple had doors also at the entrance, and lintels over them, of the same height with the Temple itself. They were adorned with embroidered veils, with their flowers of purple, and pillars interwoven: and over these, but under the crown-work, was spread out a golden vine, with its branches hanging down from a great height, the largeness and fine workmanship of which was a surprising sight to the spectators, to see what vast materials there were, and with what great skill the workmanship was done. (Josephus, Ant Book XV Part 2)

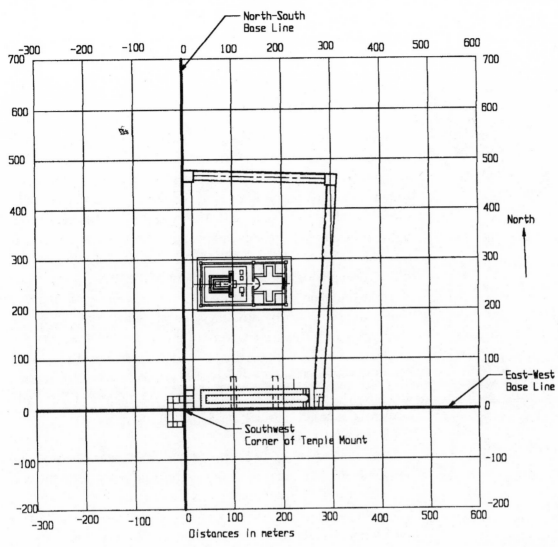

Figure 6-5
Temple Mount grid

helped the builders decide how much to cut or fill for the foundations of the retaining walls.

Excavation

The next phase of work was excavating a foundation for new retaining walls. When the site survey was completed, hundreds of laborers began to clear the vegetation along the staked outline of the Temple Mount. They used shovels, picks, and hoes to remove trees and brush. Excavation crews cut a wide trench through the topsoil to bedrock. Then they loosed and loaded the soft soil with ox-drawn plows onto carts, shown in Figure 6-6. Where they found exposed bedrock, the stonecutters used iron picks to cut the soft limestone free.

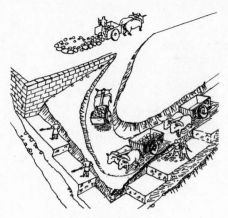

Figure 6-6
Excavating Temple Mount foundations

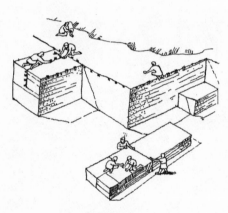

Figure 6-7
Quarrymen cutting level planes

Each cart carried about eight cubic yards of rubble, weighing ten tons. Teams of oxen pulled the loaded carts for backfilling the space inside the great retaining walls.

Wall Construction

In some places, bedrock was 30 to 40 feet below grade and it was necessary to excavate deep trenches through the overburden. When the bedrock was exposed, the grading crews widened the trench to allow quarrymen to cut the rock into level horizontal planes, as shown in Figure 6-7. They did this by cutting grooves in the rock and filling them with water to be sure that the planes were level. Where the top of bedrock sloped, they stepped the foundation planes along the alignment of the walls.

Then they laid giant undressed stones as the retaining wall foundation. Finally, the stonemasons placed dressed stones in courses to form the substructure of the wall. See Figure 6-8.

Where they had to cut bedrock deeply, stonecutters established quarries. They cut the bedrock into blocks and dressed and stored them to be used later in construction of the walls. Some of the largest stone blocks used in the lower courses were cut from nearby bedrock.

Large undressed stone blocks formed the lower courses. The stonemasons constructed the upper exposed portions of the wall of dressed ashlars. Each course was about two cubits (36 inches) in height. Mortar was not necessary between the stone blocks; each stone was so accurately finished for close contact that the coefficient of friction provided the stability of the wall. Joints were almost invisible to the eye. The masons finished the top and bottom surfaces of each block into parallel planes. Some of the lower courses near the northeast corner of the Temple Mount were composed of 4-foot-high and 23-foot-long stone blocks.

Since misalignment between the top and bottom planes was difficult to correct, stonecutters used wooden squares and measuring rods to maintain accurate right angles of the block faces. They bonded smaller stone blocks together by inserting iron I- or U-shaped clamps into chiseled slots, and poured molten lead around the clamps to lock them in place.

Above grade, the exposed face of each stone block had smooth margins and rough interior, projecting about ¾ inch.

Stonemasons battered, or sloped, the outer face of the retaining wall inward as it rose. They set back each succeeding course about one inch from the course below it. Therefore, the top face of the completed wall was about 2½ feet farther back than the bottom. This batter provided both structural and architectural benefits to the work (Ben-Dov 49). Tilting the wall backward provided greater resistance to the earth pressure behind it. Figure 6-9 shows a section through the wall from bedrock to top of the retaining wall.

Southern Wall

The Southern Wall, the highest of the four walls, was about 912 feet long. Figure 6-10 shows its elevation. This wall was built on the *Ophel,* or the high point of the ridge that separated the *Tyropoeon Valley* from the *Kidron Valley.* Because the wall crossed part of the valley, a principal watercourse, the stonemasons constructed a storm drain through it to allow water to pass through.

They installed 35 courses of ashlars at the southeast corner, giving it a spectacular height of 138 feet above bedrock. Because of its height, the top of the wall was the place from where a trumpeter called the people to service, as shown in Figure 6-11. An inscribed stone parapet at the top of the wall spelled out these words (Biblical Archaeology Society):

To the place of trumpeting . . .

Gates in the Southern Wall
Two major gates, known as the *Huldah Gates,* pierced the Southern Wall of the Temple Mount. These served as the entrance to a 63-foot-long, 5-foot-wide, and 11½-foot-high tunnel that led north through underground chambers and up to the plaza level.

The western of these two gates was known as The Double

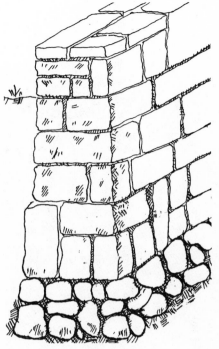

Figure 6-8
Stone wall

Figure 6-9
Section through Temple Mount

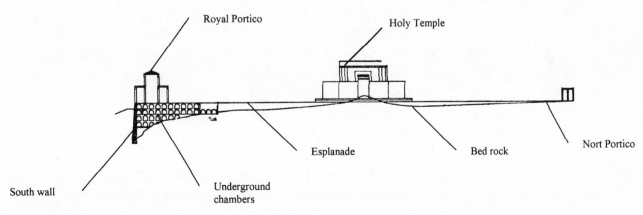

Royal Portico

Holy Temple

Esplanade

Bed rock

Nort Portico

South wall

Underground
chambers

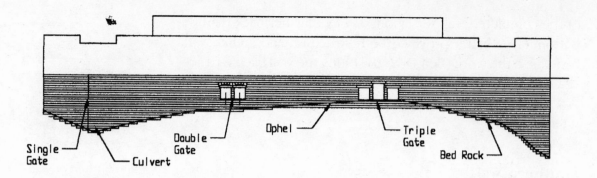

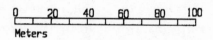

Figure 6-10
Southern Wall elevation

Gate or Western Huldah Gate. It was 43 feet wide and 8½ feet long, including a center pier, and it led to a tunnel and ramp. This entrance also went up to the *Court of the Gentiles* on the esplanade. A relieving arch that capped this gate was a combination of a semi-elliptical arch and a massive lintel. Inside, a double-vaulted vestibule led to an ascending passageway. Figure 6-12 shows the Double Gate in the Southern Wall.

The Triple Gate (or Eastern Huldah Gate) was about 50 feet wide and contained three portals—a broad center opening and two smaller ones. A stone lintel spanned the head of each opening. This gate also led to a passageway for access to the esplanade. Inside the passageway were two 5-foot, 9-inch–diameter monolith columns. Figure 6-13 shows an elevation of this gate.

Plaza and Staircase

A grand monumental staircase led from the Huldah Gates down to a lower plaza. The steps were cut from the bedrock and paved with flat stones. This 215-foot-wide stairway had 30 steps, each 7 to 10 inches high and 12 to 36 inches wide. This design required the pilgrims to ascend and descend in a slow and deliberate manner. To reach the esplanade, the public had to climb these steps, enter one of the gates, and walk through inclined tunnels.

Western Wall

Figure 6-11
Blowing the shofar from the pinnacle

Herod's masons built the entire Western Wall outside and roughly parallel to the preexisting Western Wall. To make it more defendable, Herod ordered that the wall start at the bottom of the Tyropoeon Valley. His workers set huge stone blocks in the lower courses, then his masons installed nine courses of stone ashlars over the immense foundation blocks. Some of these huge blocks formed the outside wall of a larger water reservoir under the esplanade.

Josephus described the completed Western Wall as follows:

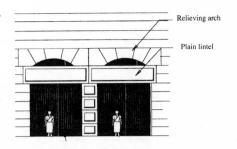

Figure 6-12
Double Gate at Southern Wall

And it was a structure more noteworthy than any under the sun. For while the depth of the ravine was great, and no one who bent over to look into it from above could bear to look down to the bottom, the height of the portico standing over it was so very great, that if anyone looked down from its rooftop, combining the two elevations, he would become dizzy and his vision would be unable to reach the end of so measureless depth. (Ant 15:412)

The Western Wall, which faced the city of Jerusalem, was pierced with viaducts, arch bridges, and gates. These included *Warren's Gate, Robinson's Arch, Barclay's Gate, Wilson's Arch, Fourth Gate,* and the *Single Gate.* All used an arch like that shown in Figure 6-14.

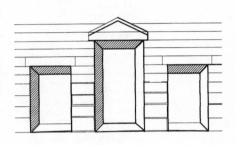

Figure 6-13
Triple Gate at Southern Wall

There were thirteen courses of ashlars between the esplanade level and the threshold of Barclay's Gate, and an additional fourteen courses to bedrock. The total height was approximately 101 feet.

Warren's Gate

A 27-foot-long stone lintel capped Warren's Gate. This lintel was 70 feet high and about 5 feet thick, and it weighed about 70 tons. Figure 6-15 shows a view of Warren's Gate.

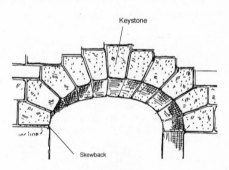

Figure 6-14
Typical stone arch

Robinson's Arch

Robinson's Arch was the abutment for a stairway over the Tyropoeon Street that led to a gateway on the Western Wall. The lintel over this gateway was about 25 feet wide and about 9 feet high. The threshold of the gateway was the lowest of all the gates along this wall.

Barclay's Gate

Barclay's Gate (or *Coponius* or *Kiphonoe Gate*) was north of the Robinson Arch. This gate was the entrance to a ramp that led up to the esplanade. Figure 6-16 shows an elevation and section

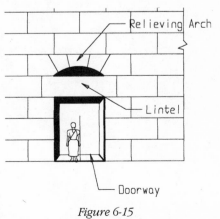

Figure 6-15
Warren's Gate

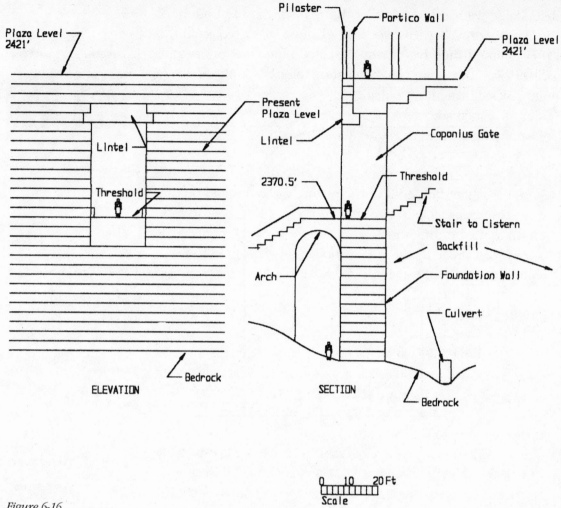

Figure 6-16
Coponius or Barclay's Gate

through this gate. The opening was about 33 feet high and 20 feet wide. The lintel was 25 feet long and 7 feet high. Access to this gate was over an arch ramp and stairway from the main street.

Wilson's Arch

Wilson's Arch was the last of a series of stone arches that supported a causeway spanning the Tyropoeon Valley. This arch, 43 feet wide, spanning 42 feet, was 72 feet above the bedrock level of the valley. This causeway, or aqueduct, brought water by gravity to the Temple Mount from the *Ein-Etam* spring (Mazar 217; Cornfeld 1982, 177). Access to the esplanade was directly from the bridge through the West Portico. Figure 6-17 shows an elevation of this arch. Figure 6-18 shows the *voussoirs* (truncated wedge-shaped pieces of an arch) and other parts.

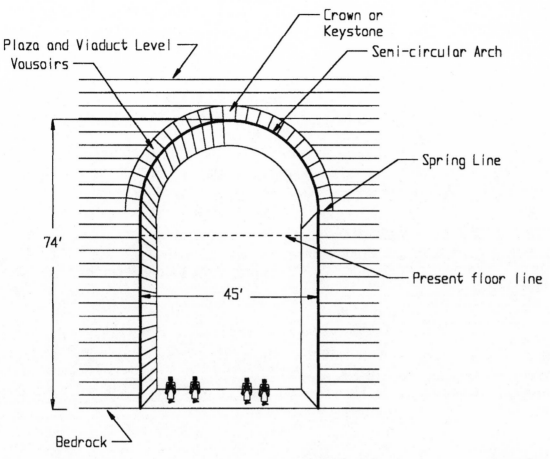

Figure 6-17
Wilson's Arch

Fourth Gate

History records very little about the Fourth Gate; Josephus described it as being in the Western Wall opposite the Temple area.

Tyropoeon Street

The Tyropoeon Street was the main north–south road parallel to the base of the Western Wall. This roadway was paved with uniformly thick, rectangular, flat limestone slabs over the bottom of the Tyropoeon Valley. Builders also constructed small shops, made of stone blocks, between the roadway and the Western Wall.

Tunnels

Herod's engineers carved tunnels under the Tyropoeon Street and the Temple Mount to carry away storm and waste water. One drainage tunnel, 550 feet long and 20 feet below the roadway, was hewed from the bedrock and capped as a continuous barrel vault.

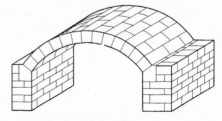

Figure 6-18
Parts of a masonry arch

A second drainage tunnel started at a vaulted room supporting the narrow street along the Southern Wall. This tunnel, constructed of stone blocks, was 3 feet wide, 11½ feet high, and 70
feet long.

Eastern Wall

Herod's builders could not extend the Temple Mount eastward,
because the Solomonic and Hasmonean walls were built to the
very edge of a steep slope to the *Kidron Valley.*

Golden Gate

The Golden Gate was located along the Eastern Wall of the Temple Mount, 1,023 feet north of the southeast corner.

Susa Gate

Susa Gate, or Shushan Gate, was east of the temple area and led
to an underground corridor below the level of the Single Gate.
There is some question as to whether this or the Golden Gate is
to be identified with the *Beautiful Gate* mentioned in Acts 3:2,
10.

Northern Wall

The north side of the Temple Mount was the least defendable of
the four walls. Because there were no adjacent valleys for protection, Herod's workers excavated an artificial valley (*fosse*) to
defend the Temple Mount from the north. In addition, Herod enlarged the *Fortress Antonia* at the northwest corner to garrison
Roman troops. He also built a tower at the eastern corner of the
wall. The combination of the *fosse,* fortress, and tower provided
better protection against a hostile attack from the north.

Tadi Gate

The *Tadi Gate* was approximately at the center of the Northern
Wall of the Temple Mount. There is little known about this gate.

Backfilling the Temple Mount

As Herod's masons raised the retaining walls course by course,
they backfilled and compacted the space within the walls with
earth and rubble. This fill material was transported by carts and
discharged in even layers. As each layer was placed, they added

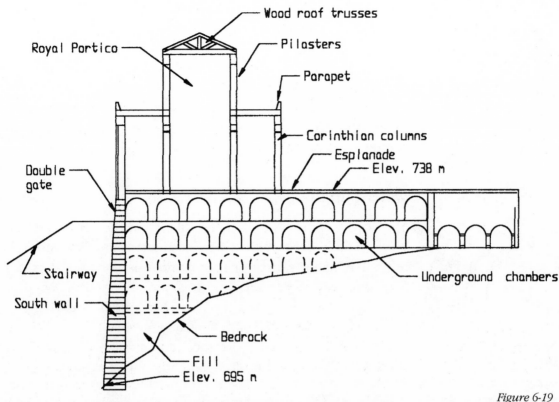

Figure 6-19
Section through Royal Portico

> He also encompassed the entire Temple with very large cloisters, contriving
> them to be in a due proportion thereto; and he laid out larger sums of money
> upon them than had been done before him, till it seemed that no one else had
> so greatly adorned the Temple as he had done. There was a large wall to both
> the cloisters, which wall was itself the most prodigious work that was ever
> heard of by man. The hill was a rocky ascent that declined by degrees
> towards the east parts of the city, until it came to an elevated level. (Josephus,
> Ant Book XV Chapter III)

water and compacted the fill by rolling heavy stone drums. Oxen
trampled over the backfill for further compaction to make the fill
as dense as possible for support of the esplanade's paving and
buildings.

Underground Chambers and Vaults

Along with the backfilling operation, workers simultaneously
constructed new subterranean chambers, vaults, and tunnels.
Some structures were cut out of solid rock and others were of
vaulted arches. In one tunnel, they built two sides of stacked
stone ashlars supporting an arched roof constructed of *voussoirs.*

At the southeastern part of the Temple Mount they constructed four levels of chambers. Figure 6-19 shows how they

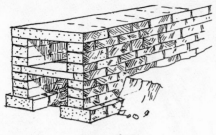

Figure 6-20
Stone aqueduct

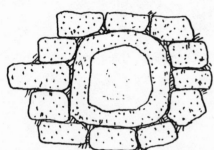

Figure 6-21
Stone syphon conduit

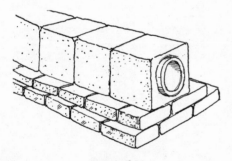

Figure 6-22
A stone pipe

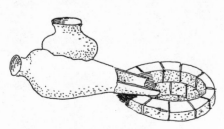

Figure 6-23
Discharge of rainwater into a cistern

built each chamber with arched vaults about 20 feet wide and 20 feet high. The floor of the upper chambers was approximately 20 feet below the esplanade paving. They filled spaces between the underground chambers and enclosing walls with earth and rock to form a level podium.

They used these underground chambers as storerooms. Later, during the Crusader Period they were used as stables and re-named *Solomon's Stables* (Cornfeld 1982, 351).

Water Supply

The water supply system for Jerusalem and the Temple Mount was as bold in design and as well executed as most modern systems. The major source of pure water was the three *Pools of Solomon.* A stone conduit from this pool followed the contour line to conduct water into the city. This conduit was about 13 miles long and dropped approximately 54 feet. The pools were fed by sealed fountains above them and another conduit along the *Wadi Urtas.* Josephus described this system as follows:

> Pilate, the Procurator of Judea, undertook to bring a current of water to Jerusalem, and did it with the sacred money, and derived the origin of the stream from the distance of 200 furlongs. (Ant 18:60)

To construct this conduit, Herod's workers cut tunnels through hills near Bethlehem and the *Valley of Hinnon* above the *Lower Pool of Gihon.* The conduit led around the southern end of Mount Zion and reached the city at an altitude of 2,420 feet on the west side of the Tyropoeon Valley. Figure 6-20 shows a typical water conduit.

Another water conduit served as a siphon (Figure 6-21) across a hollow near *Rachel's Tomb.* The lowest part of the siphon was 100 feet below its ends. It was 15 inches in diameter and made of blocks of stone shaped with collar and socket joints. After placement, the conduit was covered with rubble and cement for strength and protection. Figure 6-22 illustrates such a conduit.

The main sources of running water for the Temple Mount was two springs in the Kidron Valley—*Springs of the Mother of Steps* and the *Wells of Job.* The latter was south of the two ridges and difficult to defend in time of trouble.

The priests used rainfall as an important water source. Water was collected from the esplanade and roofs and carried by clay or lead pipes to cisterns. Figure 6-23 shows rainwater being discharged into a typical cistern under construction.

Reservoirs and Cisterns

The esplanade formed a huge rainwater catchment basin. There were at least 37 reservoirs and cisterns beneath the Temple Mount courtyard. One large reservoir, later called the *Bahr,* held 12,000 cubic meters of water. Another cistern, near Barclay's Gate, was about 9 meters below the esplanade. Figure 6-24 illustrates the construction of a cistern, and Figure 6-25 shows a completed cistern.

Following are some of the other water storage facilities:

- Pool of Israel, near the northwestern corner of the Temple Mount
- Pool of Bethesda, or Sheep's Pool, upstream and north of the Pool of Israel
- Pool of Solomon, or Silwan Pool, or Siloam Pool, near the southeast corner of the city within the walls. This pool was fed by Hezekiah's Tunnel and runoff from the Tyropoeon Valley
- Towers Pool, north of Herod's Palace, fed by an aqueduct from the west
- Pool of Hezekiah, or Snake Pool, west of the city wall in Ben Hinnon Valley

Figure 6-24
Digging a cistern

Frontius described the complexity of a Roman designed water system as follows:

> With such an array of indispensable structures carrying so many waters, compare if you will, the idle Pyramids of the useless, though famous, works of the Greeks. (Frontius, *De aquis urbis Romae;* Landels)

The Greeks based their water system on the law of gravity—*water seeks its own level*—but the Romans added scale and complexity to the system. They introduced pipes of various materials, such as wood with iron collars, clay, and lead (*plumbum*) pipes, as shown in Figure 6-26. The most common pipe size was 4 inches in diameter.

Herod's engineers were very familiar with the principle of siphons in their design of water conduits that had to cross valleys. They built both aqueducts and siphons, including inverted, U-bend, and venter siphons. They were careful to reinforce the

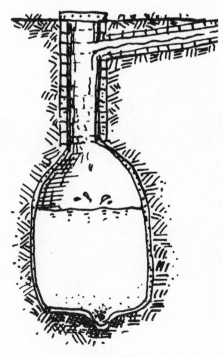

Figure 6-25
A finished cistern

*Temple Figure 6-26
Lead water pipes*

bends, as Vitruvius advised: *water pressure can break a pipe at an elbow or "knee."*

In addition to reservoirs, the Temple Mount water system included settling tanks and primary and secondary distribution centers. Outside of the Mount, sumps and pools were built at the ends of each watercourse. The main one, which was under the Tyropoeon Street, flowed to the Siloam Pool in the southern part of the City of David. Other water storage pools were built near Antonia Fortress and Herod's Palace.

Drainage Systems

Herod's engineers built two major drainage networks in Jerusalem, each at a different level. The upper-level system was just below the paving stones of the side streets. These were about 3 feet high and 5 feet wide. Both systems drained from west to east and discharged through vertical shafts 34 feet deep to a lower storm drain. The lower storm drain was under the main street in the Tyropoeon Valley and extended from Damascus Gate to Siloam Pool. It was part hewn rock and part stone arch, 3 feet wide and 6 feet high. Part of this system was built by the Hasmoneans.

When Herod's engineers found that the rocky ground under the Temple Mount was honeycombed with preexisting chambers, they enlarged and converted these cavities into cisterns. They used the rock cut from the cisterns as building material.

The most common cistern was bottle-shaped, cut into the rock 16 to 23 feet deep. The sides of the lower portion were vertical and then narrowed to the surface. The shaft opening was a cylindrical hole about 3 feet in diameter and 4½ feet deep.

Cisterns were usually located to capture rainwater from adjacent areas. A plaster coating over the interior surface prevented seepage. The plaster consisted of powdered limestone, which was similar to Portland cement. In many cisterns, a depression in the bottom caught and retained any mud or sand sediment, so that vessels dropped into the cisterns would bring up only clear water.

Hezekiah's Tunnel

The most remarkable water supply project was *Hezekiah's Tunnel*. In 701 BCE invading Assyrians threatened Jerusalem's water supply. King Hezekiah first blocked the upper outlet of *Gihon Spring,* then channeled the water down to the west side of the City of David (2 Kings 20:20; 2 Chron. 32:30). He then ordered a tunnel dug from the Spring of Gihon to a reservoir inside the city walls.

The Israelites used hammers and chisels to excavate their way through 1,750 feet of solid limestone. The upper end was only one foot higher than the outlet, with a slope of 0.6 percent grade. Two crews of miners worked simultaneously from each end, one group beginning at the Spring of Gihon, which was outside the walls of Jerusalem, and the other crew working from the Pool of Siloam. An inscription commemorating the successful tunneling was carved into the stone at the point where the two teams of miners met.

This tunnel permitted the Israelites to obtain water from the Gihon Spring during times of siege, even though the spring lay outside the city walls. The village of Siloam, located at the lowest end of the valley, was the source of water for Jerusalem mentioned in the Bible as the *Pool of Shelah* (Neh. 3:15). It was also referred to in the New Testament as the Pool of Siloam (John 9:7). The reservoir of Hezekiah was identified with the Pool of Siloam (2 Kings 20:20).

Sanitation

Sanitary wastewater was collected in plaster-lined cesspools. Toilet seats, made of a single block of limestone with holes, were set into the floor over a cesspool. Some of the toilets were made of thin stone slabs with large keyhole-shaped openings. Some toilets had two openings: The larger one went straight down to the cesspool, and the smaller one, for male urination, drained to the side. A ceramic bowl was placed beside each toilet for washing hands or pouring lime into the cesspool.

Summary

Herod's civil engineers provided an adequate water supply for the Temple Mount to last many weeks of siege. Together with the awesome retaining walls, towers, and Antonia Fortress (see Chapter 7), the Temple Mount was almost impenetrable.

Building Antonia Fortress and the Porticos

When Herod's builders completed the huge stone retaining walls, fill, and underground chambers of the Temple Mount, they began work on the four magnificent *porticos*. These structures, also known as *cloisters, stoas,* or *basilicas,* were to surround the Holy Temple. The *Royal Portico* was the largest and most elegant. It loomed over the Southern Wall and provided an expansive view of the city. The other three porticos stood above north, east and west walls. Figure 7-1 is an aerial view of the Temple Mount complex.

Antonia Fortress

Herod restored the existing Hasmonean military citadel that commanded the northwest corner of the Temple Mount. He renamed it *Fortress Antonia,* in honor of Marc Anthony. The fortress, shown on Figure 7-2, garrisoned the Roman legionnaires stationed in Jerusalem.

Figure 7-3 is a plan of this fort. Herod also used this citadel as his temporary palace (War 1:401). While some have connected this structure to the "praetorium" used later by Pontius Pilate in Jesus' trial (Matt. 27:27), the "praetorium" was much more likely to have been Herod's palace built on the western edge of the city and described by Josephus in War 1:402.

The Hasmoneans had renovated an earlier citadel that existed in the days of Nehemiah (Neh 2:8, 7:2) and that was known in Hebrew as the *Birah*. Josephus, writing in Greek, called this structure the Baris (War 1:75, 118; Ant 15:403). Figure 7-4 shows a plan view of the Temple Mount. Figure 7-5 is an aerial view looking from the northwest.

Antonia was constructed upon a 73-foot-high rock outcrop

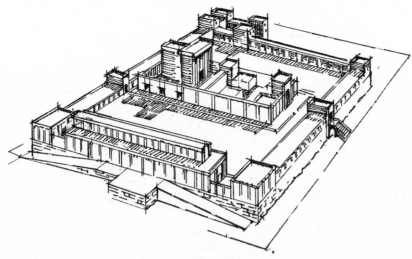

Figure 7-1
Aerial view of Temple Mount from southeast

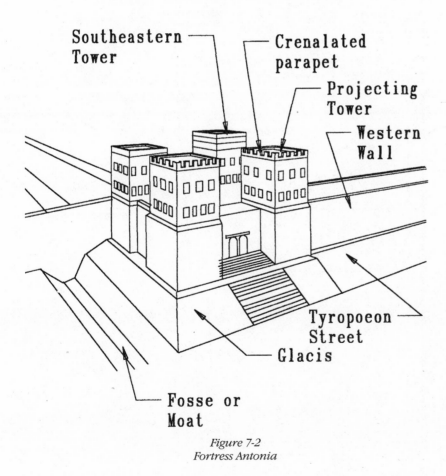

Figure 7-2
Fortress Antonia

and was located at the junction of the First and Second City Walls. The builders paved its steep embankments (*glacis*) with flagstones to resist hostile attack. Then they erected 15-foot-high walls at the top of the embankment, which joined the 70-foot

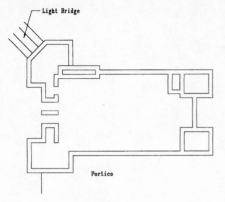

Figure 7-3
Plan of Antonia Fortress

towers of the citadel and surrounded a courtyard. The highest tower at the southeast corner, called *Straton's Tower,* provided a clear view of the temple grounds and the surrounding city.

Workmen excavated a deep moat, or *fosse,* on the north side of the fortress to provide additional protection. Then Herod's engineers built a light bridge to span the *Struthion Pool* and to provide access from the north side of the fortress to the Upper City.

Antonia Fortress and the four porticos formed a continuous defensive wall around the Temple. The main access to the fortress was by a stairway that rose from Tyropoeon Street at the west and by another stairway from the esplanade. Also a dark subterranean passageway led from the Temple area to the fortress.

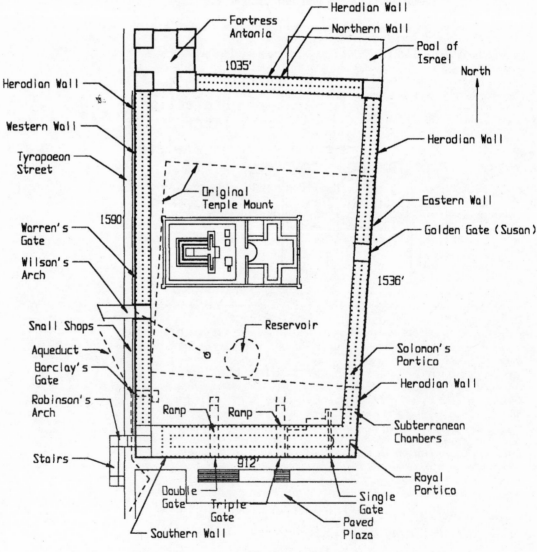

Figure 7-4
Plan of the Temple Mount

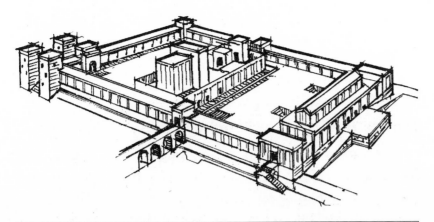

Figure 7-5
Aerial view of Temple Mount
from the southwest

Now, in the western quarter of the enclosures of the Temple there were four gates; the first led to the king's palace and went to a passage over the intermediate valley; two more led to the suburbs of the city; and the last led to the other city, where the road descended down into the valley by a great number of steps, and thence up again by the ascent; for the city lay over against the Temple in the manner of a threatre, and was encompassed with a deep valley along the entire south quarter; but the fourth front of the Temple, which was southward, had indeed itself gates in its middle, as also it had the royal cloisters, with three walks, which reached in length from the east valley unto that on the west, for it was impossible it should reach any further: and this cloister deserves to be mentioned better than any other under the sun; for while the valley was very deep, and its bottom could not be seen, if you looked from above into the depth, this farther vastly high elevation of the cloister stood upon that height, insomuch that if any one looked down from the top of the battlements, or down both these altitudes, he would be giddy, while his sight could not reach to such an immense depth. This cloister had pillars that stood in four rows one over against the other all along, for the fourth row was interwoven into the wall, which [also was built of stone]; and the thickness of each pillar was such, that three men might, with their arms extended, fathom it round, and join their hands again, while its length was twenty-seven feet, with a double spiral at its basis; and the number of all the pillars [in that court] was a hundred and sixty-two. Their chapiters were made with sculptures after the Corinthian order, and caused amazement [to the spectators], by reason of the grandeur of the whole. These four rows of pillars included three intervals for walking in the middle of this cloister; two of which walks were made parallel to each other, and were contrived after the same manner; the breadth of each of them was thirty feet, the length was a furlong, and the height fifty feet: but the breadth of the middle part of the cloister was one and a half of the other, and the height was double, for it was much higher than those on each side; but the roofs were adorned with deep sculptures in wood, representing many sorts of figures: the middle was much higher than the rest, and the wall of the front was adorned with beams, resting upon pillars, that were interwoven into it, and that front was all of polished stone, insomuch that its fineness, to such as had not seen it, was incredible, and to such as had seen it, was greatly amazing. Thus was the first enclosure. In the midst of which, and not far from it, was the second, to be gone up to by a few steps: this was encompassed by a stone wall for a partition, with an inscription, which forbade any foreigner to go in under pain of death. Now this inner enclosure had on its southern and northern quarters three gates [equally] distant from one another; but on the east quarter, towards the sunrising, there was one large gate through which such as were pure came in, together with their wives; but the Temple farther inward in that gate was not allowed to the women; but still more inward was there a third [court of the] Temple, whereinto it was not lawful for any but the priests alone to enter. The Temple itself was within this; and before that temple was the altar, upon which we offer our sacrifices and burnt-offerings to God. (Josephus, Ant Book XV Chapter XI)

The fortress complex resembled a palace within a small garrison town. It contained halls, porticos, baths, and other facilities for the Roman troops. The New Testament says that Paul took refuge here (Acts 16:23).

Corner Towers of the Temple Mount

At each corner of the Temple Mount, Herod directed his builders to construct offset-inset defense towers. These were for the priestly guards to observe all activity on the Mount. In addition to these four, they built a tower to overlook the approach of each entrance gate. Josephus described the towers in this manner:

They moreover improved this advantage of position by building four huge towers to increase the elevation from which their missiles were discharged: one to the northeast corner, the second above Xystus, the third at another corner opposite the lower town. The last was built above the roof of the priest's chambers, at the point where it was the custom of a priest to stand and give notice, by the sound of a trumpet, in the afternoon of the approach, and of the following evening of the close, of every seventh day, announcing to the people the respective hours for ceasing work and for resuming their labors. (War 4:580–583; Whiston 1979)

South Portico

A section through the South Portico *(Royal Stoa)* was shown in Figure 6-19. It was constructed with 162 monolithic white marble columns arranged in four rows forming three aisles. Each column was about 5 feet in diameter and 27 feet high, topped with a Greek Corinthian capital and having a double molded base. Figure 7-6 shows elements of the classic column.

The center aisle of the portico was 45 feet wide, and the two outside aisles 30 feet wide. The height of the center aisle, which formed a basilica, was 98 feet to the underside of the wooden roof beams. An apse at the eastern end of the basilica was where the Supreme legislative, religious, and judicial body—the Sanhedrin—met. Ceilings of the two side aisles were about 53 feet high and were ornamented with wood carvings.

The outer courts of the Royal Portico were used for assembly during pilgrimage feasts, for administration purposes, or as storerooms. Pilgrims usually assembled in the Royal Portico to

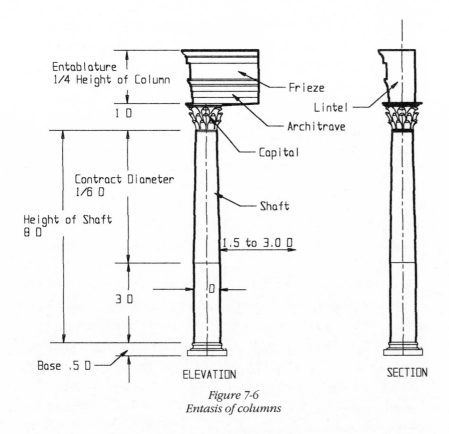

Figure 7-6
Entasis of columns

exchange foreign currency for local money and to purchase birds for religious sacrifices. Josephus described the Royal Portico as "more deserving of mention than any other under the sun" (Ant 15:412).

Carpenters constructed the roof of the Royal Portico with wood timbers and planks, which they covered with pitch to make waterproof. Unfortunately, the combination of wood and pitch was so flammable that many Jewish defenders died when the Romans set fire to this structure in 70 CE (Cornfeld 1982, 134).

West Portico

The West Portico was similar to the north and east sides of the Temple Mount. It was about 53 feet wide and contained two rows of 44-foot-high marble columns. Figure 7-7 shows a section through these porticos, described by Josephus as follows:

> The porticoes, all erected in double rows, were supported by columns 25 cubits high . . . cut from single blocks of the purest white marble . . . and the ceilings paneled with cedar . . . the porticoes were 30 cubits wide and the complete circuit of

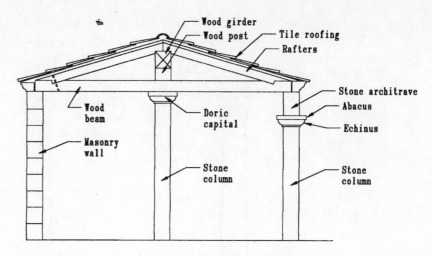

Figure 7-7
Section through portico building

them measured six furlongs, the Antonia Tower being enclosed within them. From the end to end the open court was paved with all manners of varied stones. (War 5:190–192)

East Portico

The East Portico was the oldest of the four. Josephus called it *Solomon's Portico* because it was built over the wall built by King Solomon. This building was also about 53 feet wide and contained two rows of 44-foot-high marble columns.

North Portico

The outer walls of the North Portico merged with Antonia's walls. This building, like the one on the east, was 53 feet wide and contained two rows of 44-foot-high marble columns. The *Tadi Gate* pierced this structure.

Soreg

The Soreg was a stone-lattice barrier that surrounded the consecrated area around the Temple. According to the Mishnah (Middot 2:3), the Soreg was 500 cubits (750 feet) square and 10 handbreadths (28 inches) high. However, Josephus described the Soreg as three cubits (4.5 feet) high. Its height may have been changed at different times.

Columns

The Temple Mount columns were the most attractive features of the porticos. Figure 7-8 shows how the columns supported the entablatures and the roof. Josephus wrote that the columns were thicker than the classic columns described in Vitruvius's *Ten Books on Architecture.* Each 20-foot-long monolithic column weighed about 25 tons.

It was difficult to shape the columns because they were not uniform cylinders. The diameter was smaller at the top than at the bottom. In addition, the middle of the shaft swelled (convex *entasis*). This design corrected the optical illusion that caused a straight tapered column to appear concave.

Design of colonnades was very complex and required great mathematical precision to obtain the desired optical effect. They accomplished this by:

- varying the breadth of intercolumniation
- thickening the corner columns
- grading spaces of triglyphs
- curving lines that appeared horizontal

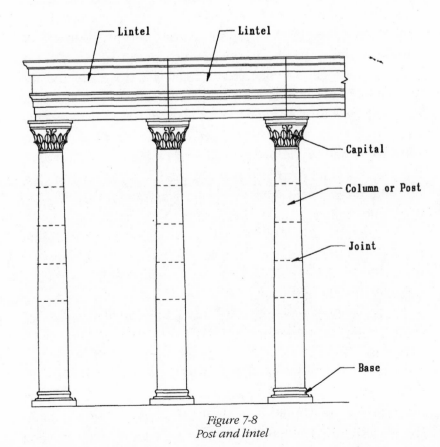

Figure 7-8
Post and lintel

- inclining lines that appeared vertical
- cambering pavements
- leaning column axis inward 6.4 cm of its height.

The stonemasons shaped the height of a column base about half of its diameter. They contracted the shaft of the column one-sixth of its diameter to the capital. They designed the stone entablature, shown being lifted in Figure 7-9, including the lintel and cornice, to be equal to one-quarter of the entire height of the column, including its base, shaft, and capital. They usually decorated the entablature with bands of eggs-and-darts and dentils, as shown in Figure 7-10 (A. D. Hamlin 1904).

Figure 7-9
Riggers lifting an entablature

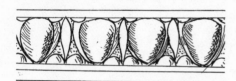

Figure 7-10
Detail of egg-and-dart design

Orders

At the time of Herod, the most commom styles, or orders, of building columns were the Doric, Ionic, and Corinthian. The capitals, shafts, bases, and proportions of each style were different from each other. In the Etruscan Doric order, the height of the column was seven times its diameter, while the height of the Greek Doric column was eight times its diameter. In Greek Corinthian style, the ratio was normally nine diameters. These columns were more slender than those used in the porticos, which Josephus described as five diameters.

Except for small columns and those used in the porticos of the Temple Mount, columns were usually segmental. The stonemasons built cylindrical segments that they could easily handle. They made up a 30- to 40-foot shaft of ten to twelve drums. They built some Doric and Corinthian capitals with two segments, doweling the parts together with iron pegs. In the Doric capital, the cone part and the cap were separate pieces. The column base was also a separate segment, fixed to the foundation with iron dowels.

To lock in the dowels, stonecutters chiseled square holes into the drums, inserted bronze or iron bars, then poured in molten lead. They prepared the column sections to fit tightly together by grinding the adjacent planes precisely.

The entablature consisted of an ornate stone lintel that spanned columns and supported the roof. See Figure 7-11. The craftsmen locked the lintels to the column capitals so that they would not shift. The span of the lintel was limited to about five times its depth; otherwise, it would tend to crack. Therefore, a two-cubit (3-feet) deep lintel could span about 10 cubits (15 feet). Column spacing also varied with different building styles *(orders),* ranging

Figure 7-11
Setting a stone lintel

between one and a half to three times the column diameter. They constructed the exterior portico walls with built-in rectangular pillars *(pilasters),* which projected out about one-half their width.

Various orders of columns resembled the human form. The Doric column was like the human male figure and the Ionic column was that of a female figure. Extending the height of the shaft produced a more slender and graceful appearance. Volutes (spirals) in the Ionic capital represented a woman's hair, and the fluted shaft appeared as folds in her garments. The base of the Ionic column resembled the twisted cords of her sandals. See Figure 7-12 for a typical Ionic column.

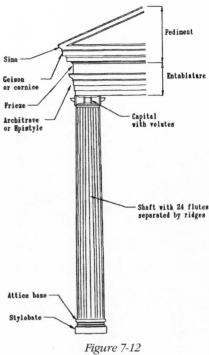

Figure 7-12
Ionic column

Arches

Herod's builders used stone arches extensively in the viaducts, tunnels, and underground chambers of the Temple Mount. Romans were the first to use the arch (De Camp 1965, 90). Before the arch, builders relied mainly on post and lintel construction, but masonry arches permitted larger openings and room sizes. Criterion for the design of arches has changed very little through the ages.

Components of an arch were the *skewback,* located at the spring line; *extrados,* which formed the arch; and the *keystone* at the crown. Figure 7-13 shows how an arch was supported during its construction (A. D. Hamlin 81).

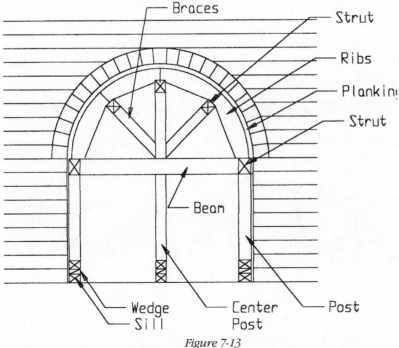

Figure 7-13
Centering for support of an arch

Figure 7-14
A vaulted arch

The barrel vault, shown in Figure 7-14 was a type of arch useful in large rooms, aqueducts, and bridges. It was built of semicircular forms as in Wilson's Arch. A groined arch, shown in Figure 7-15, is one in which two barrel arches intersect.

In the construction of the arch, stone blocks spanned an opening by transferring the vertical loads laterally to adjacent blocks and to the supports. Three conditions were necessary to ensure stability.

- Elevation of the ends must remain unchanged.
- Inclination of the skewback must be fixed.
- Length of span must remain constant.

If any of these conditions were violated by sliding, settling, or rotating, the arch would fail. Ancient engineers followed these criteria for building a safe arch. They may have used the Line of Thrust or Graphic Analysis Method to calculate the dimensions of the arch, as do modern structural engineers.

Ornamentation

The fear of idolotry as specified in Exodus 20:4, "Thou shalt not make thee any graven image," and Exodus 20:5, "Thou shalt not bow down to them and thou shalt not serve them," were implied prohibition against the human form in ornamentation (Sed-Rajna). Nevertheless, Herod was able to use a wide range of ornamentation.

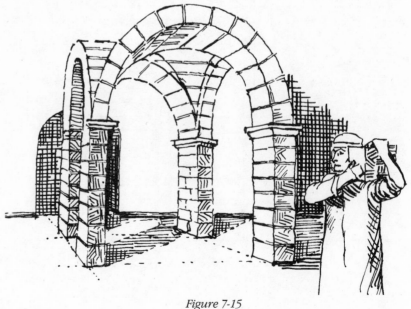

Figure 7-15
A groined arch

- Bulls
- Palm trees (life trees)
- Ethrogs (citron fruit)
- Lulav (branches of the palm)
- Acanthus leaves (see Figure 7-16)
- Egg-and-dart
- Ram's horn
- Lion of Judea
- Three crowns
- Seven-branched candlesticks (the menorah)
- Jachin and Boaz (columns)
- Six-pointed stars (Star of David)
- Zodiacal signs
- Anchors
- Chalices
- Cherubim (sphinx-like figures with a woman's head, lion's body, and large wings)

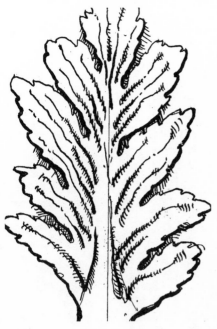

Figure 7-16
Acanthus leaf

Summary

The structures that surrounded the Holy Temple provided protection, administration, and shelter for visitors and permanent Temple personnel. The Antonia Fortress, towering over the northwest corner, was a small citadel that served as a garrison for Roman soldiers and priestly guards and as a temporary palace for King Herod. The porticos on the north, east, and west sides of the great plaza provided shelter for Temple visitors. The Royal Portico that towered over the southern wall served many functions, including a meeting place for the Sanhedrin, which was the supreme Jewish legislative, religious, and judicial body. One part was for the sale of sacrificial birds of visitors.

Herod designed and built all four porticos as an extension of the Temple Mount's defensive walls. There were observation towers at corners and battlements from which archers and spear throwers could resist any attackers.

The fortress and porticos were designed to conform to the latest and best Roman architectural styles. The buildings were so beautiful that Josephus described them as "more deserving of mention than any under the sun."

CHAPTER 8

The Temple and Courts

King Herod wanted his Holy Temple to be larger and more magnificent than Solomon's Temple. Scholars conventionally refer to Solomon's Temple as the "First Temple," and the one rebuilt by the returning exiles from Babylonia under Zerubbabel as the "Second Temple," with Herod's construction being merely a renovation of the latter. Some have argued, however, that because Herod's renovations were so extensive, it would be more appropriate to consider his edifice a "Third Temple." While this is certainly a reasonable assertion, the convention still holds to refer to both the Temples of Zerubbabel and Herod collectively as the "Second Temple." Figures 8-1 through 8-5 are illustrations of Solomon's Temple. Figure 8-1 shows an aerial view. Figure 8-2 shows the east view. Figure 8-3 shows a cross-section, and Figure 8-4 is a longitudinal section. Figure 8-5 gives a floor plan of the Temple.

The measurements given in this chapter are approximate because of the lack of precision of the time, the various lengths of a cubit (15 to 23 inches), and the many translations over the years. The dimensions and plan layout are schematic.

Solomon's Temple

Because of its flat rock and prevailing winds, a Jebusite farmer named *Araunah* chose the future site of the Temple Mount as a grain-threshing floor (2 Sam. 24:24–25). In the parallel version of this episode in 2 Chron. 3:1, the Jebusite farmer is called Ornan, and the site is called Mount Moriah, thereby connecting it with the place of the Binding of Isaac in Genesis 22. David, King of the Israelites, purchased the land from *Araunah* for fifty shekels and built an altar upon the rock (2 Sam. 24:18–25). Although David hoped to build a permanent *House for the Lord* on this site, his son Solomon carried out the plan.

In about 952 BCE, King Solomon constructed the *House of God* on top of Mount Moriah. His Temple was part of a complex that included a royal palace and several other structures. The sanctuary showed the influence of the nearby Egyptian and Mesopotamian religious architecture. Its plan had strong similarities to the New Kingdom temples of Egypt, which consisted of three parts: the inner sanctuary for the cult statue, the hypostyle hall, and the outer courtyard for the public.

Solomon's artisans built the walls of this holy edifice of large limestone blocks and the flat roof of wood beams, cedar planks, and asphalt. Like many other temples in the ancient Near East, the structure stood on layers of large stone slabs. In addition to their architectural effect, the heavy stone mat provided a stable foundation that could withstand earthquakes. They also served to raise the floor of the building above the surrounding esplanade level.

The First Temple had inner and outer courts and surrounding chambers. The inner sanctuary *(Debir),* also known as "the Holy of Holies," was a small, dark, raised room that contained the *Ark of the Covenant,* which held the tablets of the *Ten Commandments,* the most treasured sacred object of the Jews. As with its Egyptian counterpart, only the High Priest could enter the Holy of the Holies and under the purist of conditions.

A rectangular hall *(Hechal)* stood before the *Debir.* This room, which resembled the form in Hittite temples, was the priestly ritual center of the Temple. A row of small windows near the ceiling in the north and south walls illuminated the chamber. The interior had no exposed stones; the walls were completely covered with durable, sweet-smelling cedar and cypress planks. The ceiling was covered with ornamental, sunken wooden panels.

The Porch *(Ulam)* was the outermost chamber of the sanctuary. Two 18-cubit (27-foot) high bronze pillars, called *Jachin* and *Boaz,* flanked its doorway, which faced the east. They symbolized the relationship between the monarchy and the Temple.

It is believed that the Temple was 70 cubits (105 feet) long, 20 cubits (30 feet) wide, and 30 cubits (45 feet) high. Perhaps because of purity considerations, the Bible says that the stoneworkers for Solomon's Temple used unique methods of construction:

> . . . there was neither hammer nor axe nor any tool of iron heard in the house, while it was in building. (1 Kings 6:7).

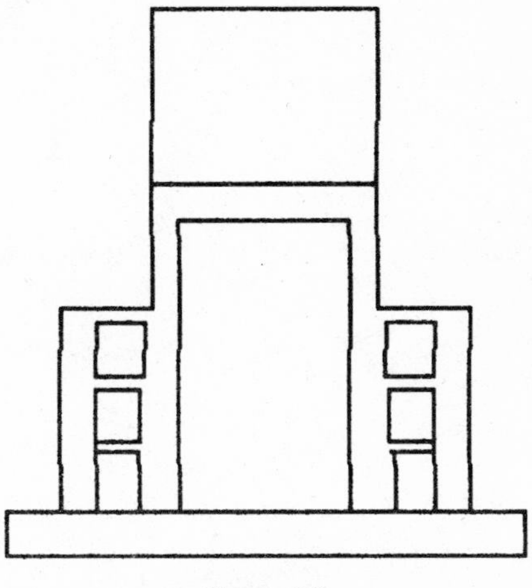

Therefore, it appears that they connected the wooden roof beams with wooden pegs and dressed the stones away from the building site. The description continued as follows:

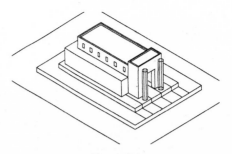

Figure 8-1
Aerial view of Solomon's Temple

Figure 8-2
East view of Holy Temple

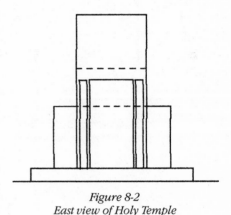

Figure 8-3
Cross-section through Holy Temple

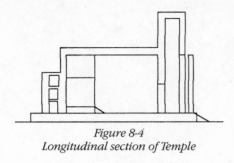

Figure 8-4
Longitudinal section of Temple

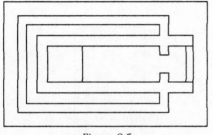

Figure 8-5
Floor plan of Holy Temple

And he carved all the walls of the house round about with carved figures of cherubim and palm-trees and open flowers . . . (1 Kings 6:29)

And for the house he made windows broad within, and narrow without. (1 Kings 6:4)

. . . and he covered in the house with planks of cedar over beams. (1 Kings 6:9)

For the entrance of the Sanctuary he made doors of olive-wood . . . (1 Kings 6:31)

And in the Sanctuary he made two cherubim of olive-wood, each ten cubits high . . . And he overlaid the cherubim with gold. (1 Kings 6:23, 28) [Cherubim were winged sphinxes with human faces.]

For the cherubim spread forth their wings over the place of the ark, and the cherubim covered the ark and the staves thereof above. (1 Kings 8:7)

The First Temple was the greatest achievement of biblical Jewish architecture to that time. Its design was based on the rituals related to it. Thousands of Israelite and Phoenician craftsmen worked on this project.

Destruction and Restoration of the Temple

Religious rituals in Solomon's Temple ended in about 586 BCE, when Nebuchadnezzar II of Babylon overran Jerusalem, destroyed the Temple, and exiled the leadership of Judah to Babylon.

About fifty years later, *Cyrus the Great* of Persia conquered Babylon and permitted the Jews to return to their homeland to restore the Temple. In 519 BCE, Jeshua, the High Priest, and Zerubbabel, the Jewish governor, directed the restoration work and tried to duplicate the original design. However, they lacked the funds to restore the building to the full glory of Solomon's time. Although there was no Royal Palace, there was a new hierarchy of courts. Much of the design of the original Temple remained intact. The Debir, Hechal, and Ulam were arranged in the same linear sequence and maintained their degrees of holiness. The Debir was located on the same sacred rock, then firmly established as a holy site.

Although similar materials were used, the two Temples were not identical, because the political and social conditions had changed. The Jews were now under the power of the Persian Empire, and Judea was a province rather than a monarchy. There

> *And now Herod, in the eighteenth year of his reign, and after the acts already mentioned, undertook a very great work, that is, to build of himself the Temple of God, and make it larger in compass, and to raise it to a most magnificent altitude, as esteeming it to be the most glorious of all his actions, as it really was, to bring it to perfection, and that this would be sufficient for an everlasting memorial of him (Josephus, Ant Book XV Chapter XI)*

Figure 8-6
East elevation of Holy Temple

was no longer a local ruler and no need for a palace or administrative complex. The partially restored temple lasted nearly 500 years before age reduced its usefulness.

Herod's Temple

Josephus described the tremendous height of Herod's Temple Mount in the following way:

> And it was a structure more noteworthy than any under the sun. For while the depth of the ravine was great, and no one who bent over to look into it from above could bear to look down to the bottom. The height of the Portico [colonnade] standing over it was so very great that if anyone looked down from its rooftop, combining the two elevations, he would become dizzy and his vision would be unable to reach the end of so measureless [or immense] depth. (Ant 15.412)

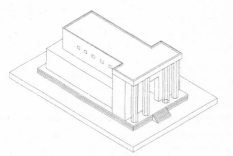

Figure 8-7
*Aerial view of Herod's Temple
from southeast*

Figures 8-6 through 8-16 illustrate Herod's Temple.

Figures 8-6 and 8-10 show the east and west elevations respectively. Figures 8-7 and 8-8 show an aerial and cutaway view, and Figure 8-9 indicates various parts of the Temple. Figure 8-11 is a longitudinal section, and Figure 8-12 is a cross-section. Figure 8-

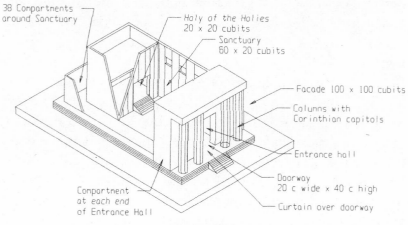

Figure 8-8
Cutaway view of Herod's Temple

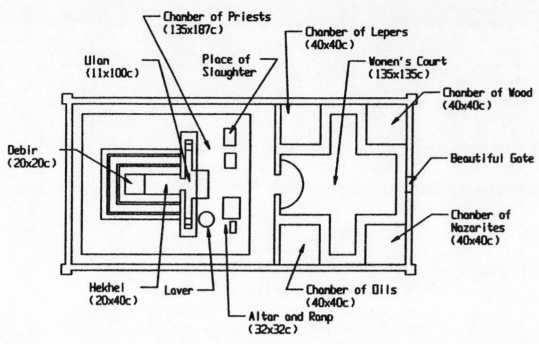

Figure 8-9
Parts of Herod's Temple

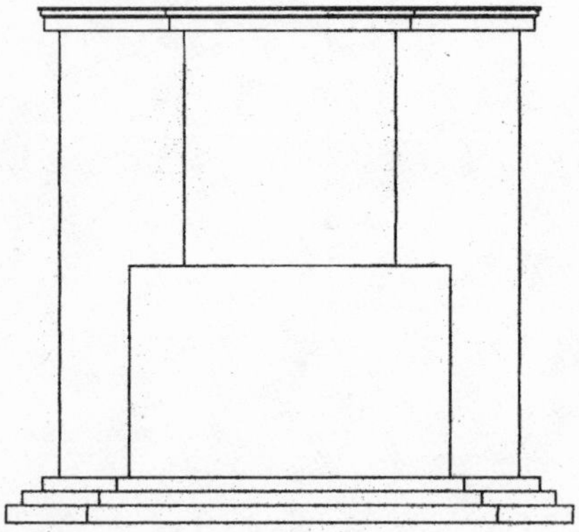

Figure 8-10
West elevation of Holy Temple

13 shows a floor plan. The Holy Temple Complex is shown in Figure 8-14, and Figure 8-15 presents a plan of the Temple Mount. Figure 8-16 illustrates the Altar at the Temple.

Herod designed the Temple to be 116 cubits (174 feet) high with a floor raised 27 cubits (40 feet) above the esplanade level. The major parts of the building remained in the same relative position as in the First Temple but more in keeping with Greek style.

Basing their design after Solomon's Temple, though this one was larger, Herod's engineers used stone from the same rock outcrop of Mount Moriah. They decorated the columns and entablatures with Corinthian capitals, grape arbors, and flowers.

Walls

Herod's engineers built the walls of large, untrimmed limestone ashlars and covered them with cedarwood on the inside and thin white marble slabs on the exterior. They reinforced the hewn stones with cedarwood beams by inserting them between every third course. These beams braced and strengthened the walls and provided support for the interior wood paneling. Workers finished the paneling without metal connections, using only wood peg, tenons, mortise, and dowels.

They covered the front and sides of the Temple with massive

> *Now the Temple was built of stones that were white and strong, and each of their length was twenty-five cubits, their height was eight, and their breadth about twelve; and the whole structure, as also the structure of the royal cloister, was on each side much lower, but the middle was much higher, till they were visible to those that dwelt in the country for a great many furlongs, but chiefly to such as lived over against them and those that approached to them. The Temple had doors also at the entrance, and lintels over them, of the same height with the Temple itself. (Josephus, Ant Book VI Chapter XI)*

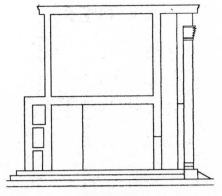

Figure 8-11
Longitudinal section through
Holy Temple

plates of gold "that flashed when the first rays of the sun hit them," according to Josephus (War 5:222).

Roof

Wooden beams, rather than pillars, carried the roof of the Temple. While Herod could not alter the dimensions of the Temple's inner sanctum, he did expand the outer building's overall size by adding small compartments for the Priests around the interior of the Sanctuary (see Sanctuary below). Doing this raised the building's height by 40 cubits (60 feet) to a total of 100 cubits (150) feet. Around the Temple's parapets were installed sharp gold spikes for ornamentation, and possibly to keep birds from fouling the building walls.

Four bronze pillars flanked the entrance doorway, each one standing two stories high. The main entrance was 40 cubits (60 feet) high and 20 cubits (30 feet) wide. Golden vines hung down from the entrance.

Ulam

The Ulam, or Porch, served as the building's entrance. At 100 cubits (150 feet) wide, it was 30 cubits (45 feet) wider than the rest of the Temple, which was only 70 cubits wide. The difference came from two wings that extended out to the north and south 15 cubits each. The Ulam's height, however, was uniform with

> *They were adorned with embroidered veils, with their flowers of purple, and pillars interwoven: and over these, but under the crown-work, was spread out a golden vine, with its branches hanging down from a great height, the largeness and the fine workmanship of which was a surprising sight to the spectators, to see what vast materials there were, and with what great skill the workmanship was done. He also encompassed the entire temple with very large cloisters, contriving them to be in a due proportion thereto; and he laid out larger sums of money upon them than had been done before him, till it seemed that no one else had so greatly adorned the temple as he had done. There was a large wall to both the cloisters; which wall was itself the most prodigious work that was ever heard of by man. (Josephus, Ant Book VI Chapter XI)*

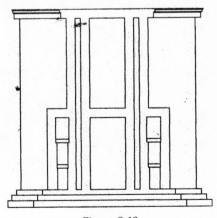

Figure 8-12
Cross-section of Holy Temple

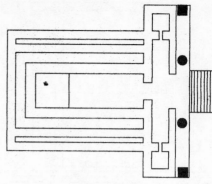

Figure 8-13
Floor plan of Holy Temple

the rest of the structure. The Ulam was about 11 cubits in depth. Because of the sharp contrast between the width of the Ulam and that of the rest of the building, the Mishnah says it was shaped like a lion (Middot 4:7), wide in the front and narrow in the back. Approach to the doors of this anteroom was via fourteen steps leading up from the Inner Court (War 5:195).

Sanctuary

The rest of the Temple was divided into two main chambers. The first of these was the Sanctuary, or Main Hall. The second is the Holy of Holies, or the *Debir,* which is described below. The Sanctuary was 70 cubits wide, including the walls, which were 5 cubits thick each, including the rows of small compartments for the Priests that surrounded the chamber. Thus the chamber itself was 20 cubits (30 feet) wide and 40 cubits (60 feet) long.

There was a total of 38 priestly compartments surrounding the Sanctuary, 15 on each side and 8 at the rear. Three storeys high, they raised the Temple's height by 40 cubits and expanded its width by 30 cubits.

Wooden beams that spanned 20 cubits (30 feet) between the two side walls supported the roof. A doorway between the Ulam and the Sanctuary, called the Royal Gate, was 20 cubits (30 feet) high and 10 cubits (15 feet) wide.

Holy of Holies

The Holy of Holies *(Debir)* was the core of the Sanctuary. This block-shaped room was 20 cubits (30 feet) square and 20 cubits (30 feet) high. A short flight of steps led up from the Sanctuary to this inner chamber. The room was curtained off, but empty. During Solomon's time, the Debir contained the Ark of the Covenant, but it was lost, perhaps during Nebuchadnezzar's destruction of the First Temple, if not earlier.

Court of the Priests

The Inner Court *(Court of Priests)* measured 209 cubits (313 feet) by 151 cubits (227 feet). The walls surrounding this court were 44 cubits (65.6 feet) high . Court of the Priests was directly in front of the Temple and included the chambers inside the outer walls. (Judaica T966). The Altar, Ramp, Place of Slaughter, and Laver were all within this court.

Altar of the Burnt Offering

A stone altar *(Altar of the Holocausts)* stood in front of the Temple. It was 53 cubits (80 feet) square and 17 cubits (25 feet) high.

Figure 8-14
Holy Temple Complex

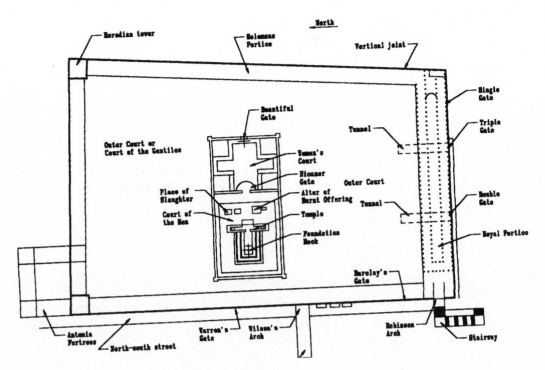

Figure 8-15
Plan of the Temple Mount

Near the altar were the slaughterhouse and tables where sacrifices were prepared (War 5:184–247). Stone for the altar was quarried from the *Beth-Cherem Valley.* (Mishnah Middot 3:4; Encyclopedia Judaica).

Court of Israel

The *Court of Israel,* or *Court of Man,* was located east of the Court of the Priests. This court measured 135 cubits (202.5 feet) by 11 cubits (16.5 feet) (Judaica T967).

Court of Women

The Court of Women was 135 by 135 cubits (202.5 by 202.5 feet) and open to the sky (Mishnah Middot 2:5). There were four 40-cubit (60-foot) square roofless chambers at the corners of this court. The chamber at the southeast corner was called *Nazarite;* the *Lepers Chamber* was at the northwest corner, and at the southwest and northeast corners were the Oil Storage chamber and the Wood Storage chamber. A gate 50 cubits (75 feet) high was on the east wall of this court.

Figure 8-16
The Altar

Court of the Gentiles

Court of the Gentiles was the name given to the entire area between the four porticos and the Temple complex.

Nicanor Gate

The *Nicanor Gate* was at the eastern entrance to the Temple complex. There were fourteen steps leading up to the two 17-cubit (25-foot) high doors. Each door was 8 cubits (11.5 feet) wide. Josephus referred to it as the *Corinthian Gate* (War 5:204), and this is another candidate for the gate referred to as the *Beautiful Gate* in Acts 3:2.

Balustrade

The balustrade, or *Soreg,* described in Chapter 7, was a low lattice wall that marked the border of the inner sanctuary. The wall contained pillars, or plaques of carved stone (stelae), set along the perimeter of the balustrade. These were inscribed in Greek and Latin, warning the public that no foreigner should enter the sacred grounds (War 5:194, Cornfeld 1982, 177). Within this warning wall was a wall, 40 cubits (60 feet) high, which enclosed the entire sacred area.

Summary

The Second Temple and the Temple Mount were the most important engineered structures in the Holy Land. They represented the peak of glory of the Jewish Nation as well as the Roman Empire. Work on the Temple continued for about 80 years. Seven years after its completion, the Jews would rebel against the Romans and the Jewish War would begin.

CHAPTER 9

The Siege of Jerusalem

Although Herod thought he had made Jerusalem an impregnable fortress, it failed against the strength of the Roman Empire. The siege of Jerusalem was one of the most striking examples of military engineering in ancient times. Flavius Josephus described the battle in his *War of the Jews* based on firsthand knowledge. *Tacitus,* another Roman historian, recorded the siege in *Historiae 5:13,* and *Justus of Tiberius* also described this battle in his writings.

Background

Although the people of Jerusalem had been prosperous and productive since the Romans took control of Judea in 63 BCE, they were always on the verge of a rebellion. The seeds of rebellion were sown after Herod the Great died and his three sons each inherited a part of his kingdom. His son Archelaus ruled over Judea, the area around Jerusalem, but was such an incompetent ruler that in 6 CE he was deposed by Romans—at the request of a delegation of Jewish citizens—and Judea was placed under direct Roman rule. Groups opposed to direct Roman rule began to spring up at this time, and the situation slowly worsened as a series of Roman administrators (procurators) treated Jerusalem Jews as inferior to Romans.

Most of the 150,000 Jewish inhabitants were uncertain in their attitude toward the Romans. The *Pharisees, Sadducees,* and *Essenes* took little part in the fighting. On the other hand, the *Zealots* and some of the aristocratic priestly revolutionaries led by *Eleazar* urged forceful resistance. *John of Gischala* and *Simon bar Gioras* led the rebellion with zealous observance of the Jewish Law and militant opposition to Roman rule. They were willing to lay down their lives for independence. A few of the Zealots resorted to extreme violence and assassination, by dagger, of the Romans and their Jewish supporters. They called these terrorists *Sicarii* (Latin for "dagger men").

First Act of Rebellion

A serious incident occurred in late 40 CE, when Emperor Caligula attempted to install a statue of himself in the Holy Temple. Although Caligula died before this could be done, Jewish resentment against the Romans began to grow. To make matters worse, Judea around this time was suffering under a series of corrupt and incompetent Roman procurators. Among the worst was the last one, Gessius Florus, who provoked a riot in 66 CE when he attempted to seize money from the Temple treasury. In the course of the riot, Jewish revolutionaries in Jerusalem attacked and killed the Roman legionnaires garrisoned in the city. In reaction, the Roman governor of Syria sent the Twelfth Roman Legion to Jerusalem as a punitive force, and the War of the Jews began.

Roman Military Strength

As the Twelfth Legion entered a narrow pass near Beit Horon, Judean guerrillas ambushed and routed them. When the Romans fled, they left behind most of their catapults and siege engines. The Jews hauled the abandoned equipment back to Jerusalem and restored it. This hit-and-run attack was only a temporary Jewish victory, for they had taken on the most powerful military force in the world.

With the initial Roman military response having been repelled, Emperor Nero commissioned General Vespasian to bring a larger force to quell the rebellion. Methodically and relentlessly, Vespasian gathered three complete Roman legions (the Fifth, Tenth, and Fifteenth) along with a variety of auxiliary cohorts, so that his total force consisted of some 60,000 men.

Legion recruits were mainly Roman citizens who had enlisted for 25 years. Rome divided each 5,000- to 6000-man legion into ten *cohorts* composed of heavy infantry *(Hoplites),* combat engineers, reconnaissance, medical units, and a train of followers and freed slaves.

Heavy infantry consisted of three groups: the youngest men *(Hastati)* were usually sent to the front line; seasoned troops *(Principes)* made up the second line as backup; and the oldest men *(Triarii)* served as reserve in the rear. A line had ten battalions *(Maniples),* each with two *Centuries* of 60 to 80 men. Cavalry, archers *(sagitarii),* and light infantry *(Velites)* supported each legion.

Jewish Military Strength

Other than the priestly guards, the Jews had no formal military force. Emperor Augustus had excluded Jews from serving in the Roman Army, so few had any training. Although King Herod used Jewish and Idumaean troops to defeat the Arabs, he enlisted Babylonian Jews to police *Batanea* and *Trachonitis.* His personal bodyguards were Thracian, German, and Gaulish soldiers.

When the Roman legions first moved against the Jews, the Zealots were the only fighters. However, the aristocratic circles organized a formal army and divided the country into military districts. Josephus was in command of the Galilee and tried in vain to develop an effective military force there. Support for the rebellion in the Galilee was lukewarm, and Josephus' army quickly fell apart against Vespasian's legions. After that setback, Jewish forces gave up organized field combat and fell back into fortified cities. The last of Josephus' forces were besieged at Jotapata, and when the town eventually fell, Josephus surrendered himself to the Romans. Making the transition from military leader to historian, he accompanied the Romans throughout the rest of their campaign and recorded the events of the war for posterity.

Having subdued the Galilee, Vespasian marched west toward Jaffa and then south, subduing the Judean countryside all the way to Jericho. Having quashed the various pockets of rebellion throughout Judea, the Roman forces then directed their efforts on besieging and capturing Jerusalem.

Against this massive Roman force, the Jews relied mainly on stone walls, guerrilla warfare, archers, and hand-to-hand combat. See Figure 9-1. They had limited knowledge of large-scale field operations or strategic defense. Nevertheless, they knew the terrain and could hit and run the slower-moving legions.

Jerusalem's defenders were led by *John of Gischala, Eleazar ben Simon,* the priestly head of the Jerusalem Zealots, and *Simon bar Gioras,* the leader of the lower classes. Simon had an army of 10,000 fighters and 50 officers. James, son of Sosas, and Simon, son of Cathlas, commanded 10,000 Idumaean men and 50 officers. Eleazar and Simon, son of Arimus, led the Zealots of 2,400 men.

Figure 9-1
An archer

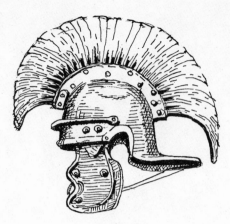

Figure 9-2
A Roman helmet

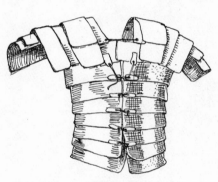

Figure 9-3
A Roman soldier's breastplate

The total number of Jewish defenders was over 24,000 fighters, including guerrilla fighters, irregulars, militant holy men, border militia, and mounted archers from Babylonia. They also had combat engineers, who repaired the captured siege engines, and artillerymen, who operated them. Their blacksmiths forged iron missiles, arrowheads, and suits of armor.

Roman Soldiers' Personal Equipment

The Roman legionnaires wore bronze or metal-covered leather helmets with hinged ear-plates. Some helmets had a projecting fin at the back and a reinforced ridge on the top. See Figure 9-2. They wore leather breastplates and backplate *(cuirass)*. Their armor consisted of overlapping thin copper or bronze sheets, or scales, attached to a fabric backing. These formed corselets that extended down to the hips. For strength, most scales had raised metal ribs and borders. See Figure 9-3.

The Roman soldiers wore heavy military boots or sandals *(caligae)* and shin guards *(greaves)* for protection of the lower part of their body. They also carried a large rectangular shield *(scutum)*, which could hide their body when they were kneeling.

They used short swords and daggers *(purgio)* for hand-to-hand combat. They also hurled javelins *(pilumae)*; these had long, four-sided pyramidal iron heads with a four-sided shank that fitted into a 6½-foot-long wooden shaft. When attacking in a tight formation, they used spears *(pilum* or *gladius)* and lances *(hasta)*.

Archers used bow and arrow for long-distance fighting. Smiths made the iron arrowheads with a barbed, three-winged *(trilobate)* form. They inserted the tang (prong), which was at the rear of the arrowhead, into a wooden shaft. The arrowheads were between ½ and 2 inches long and ½ to ¾ inch wide at the tip of the barbs. An iron arrowhead was relatively soft but could kill a man who was protected only by leather. Some arrowheads were made of hardened steel and could pierce copper or bronze armor.

Soldiers of the auxiliary forces were protected with shirts of armor, a helmet, a smaller and lighter oval shield, and heavy military boots or sandals. Each man carried a long narrow blade lance *(lancea)*, sword *(spatha)*, and dagger.

Figures 9-4 and 9-5 show the personal equipment of the Roman soldier.

The footmen are armed with breastplates and headpieces, and have swords on each side; but the sword which is upon their left side is much longer than the other; for that on the right side is not longer than a span. Those footmen also that are chosen out from among the rest to be about the general himself have a lance and a buckler; but the rest of the foot-soldiers have a spear and a long buckler, besides a saw and a basket, a pick-axe and an axe, a thong of leather, and a hook, with provisions for three days; so that a footman hath no great need of a mule to carry his burdens. The horsemen have a long sword on their right sides and a long pole in their hand: a shield also lies by them obliquely on one side of their horses, with three or more darts that are borne in their quiver, having broad points, and no smaller than spears. They have also headpieces and breastplates, in like manner as have all the footmen. (Josephus, Wars Book III Chapter V)

Figure 9-4
A Roman legionnaire

Defense of Jerusalem

The Jewish defenders protected the city by a series of massive stone walls and towers, designed and constructed by military engineers. The First Wall and Second (Middle) Wall had been built by the Hasmoneans, and the Third Wall (Outer Wall) had been built by Herod. Most walls were about 36 feet high and had towers at strategic intervals and at each gateway. There were ninety towers in the Third Wall and fourteen in the Middle Wall. The First Wall was 4 miles long and had sixty towers. The towers dominated essential locations and provided a good field-of-fire. These fortifications were to foil the efforts of sappers, since the Jews respected the Roman engineers' ability to breach the walls.

Jewish defenders stocked the tops of the walls and towers with arrows, rocks, and combustible material, such as wood, pitch, and oil. They would hurl these down on the attackers as they approached the walls.

The main defense of the Temple was its stone walls, which protected the Mount from three sides. The Antonia Fortress and a system of *glacis* and *fossae* defended the north side. See Figure 8-12 in Chapter 8.

However, in spite of the careful design and construction, the walls were only as good as the defenders. If the Jewish fighters behind the walls faltered, the fortifications themselves could not prevent the enemy from coming through.

Walls of Jerusalem

The oldest walls were the Ophel Walls surrounding the City of David; these were partially built by the Jebusites, King David, King Solomon, and King Herod. The First Wall started from Herod's Palace to Wilson's Arch and then went southeast to the

City of David. This wall separated the Upper City from the Lower City. The Second Wall, built by the Hasmoneans, also started at Herod's Palace and extended to the Antonia Fortress. This wall encircled Tyropaeon Valley and the market area and protected the city proper. The Third Wall encircled Bezetha, the Wood Market, and the Sheep Market. Other defensive walls were part of Antonia Fortress and the porticos of the Temple Mount.

Since 2000 BCE, building defensive stone walls had become an art. Engineers constructed the walls for permanence, resistance to battering rams, and dismantling by sappers. Solomon's walls were about 15 feet thick and 14 feet high; they were built of undressed *(cyclopean)* stone and strengthened with buttresses. The later walls were constructed with dressed stone. Figure 9-6 shows the general construction of a fortified wall.

Casemate walls consisted of two walls, the outer one about 6 feet thick and the inner 4 feet thick. A 10-foot space with cross walls formed chambers between the walls. These were used for storerooms, guardrooms, armories, and living quarters. During attack, these rooms were filled with rubble in the lower levels, making penetration more difficult.

Walls also served as firing platforms to shoot down on attackers. Crenelated (serrated) stone parapets allowed archers to fire their bows through the gaps and then hide behind the projections. In some places there were wooden shields so the defenders could stand while shooting. Cantilevered wooden platforms projecting out from the parapets stored combustibles, which could be set afire and dropped upon enemy soldiers below.

Wall Gates

Gates were the weakest points of a wall. Single gates accommodated people, but carts and wagons required double gates. The gate doors swung on posts anchored into a lintel at the top and set into a stone socket at the bottom. Doors were made of heavy timbers and locked with metal bolts.

Because gates were the weak link in a city's defenses, ancient engineers over the centuries devised ways to protect them against enemy onslaughts. Towers and recessed chambers built within the gates provided an easy line of fire on who tried to rush through the gate. Engineers built straight gateways for carts and chariots and right-angle gateways for the other wall openings.

Figure 9-5
A Roman soldier

With the gate at a right angle to the wall, attackers could not charge through it with any great speed. See Figure 9-7.

Defensive Measures

With the Roman Army coming, the city defenders prepared all approaches to the walls to hamper the attack. These defenses included *glacis, moats (fossae),* and earth ramparts. Glacis were an inclined stone surface placed over layers of beaten earth forming a steep slope at the bottom of a wall. See Figure 9-8. They dug

Figure 9-6
Section through a fortified wall

> *They also erect four gates. one at every side of the circumference, and those large enough for the entrance of the beasts, and wide enough for making excursions, if occasion should require. (Josephus, Wars Book III Chapter V)*

moats in front of the glacis. Their first line of defense was a rampart made of layers of rock and tamped earth.

Engineers built the wall foundations deep with large stones to prevent undermining and to enable it to withstand the impact of the battering ram. The size of the stones diminished toward the top of the wall. They made the joints as small as possible to prevent sappers from prying the stones loose. The glacis hampered placement of scaling ladders or towers next to the wall. Rampart and moats prevented battering rams or siege towers to be moved close to the wall.

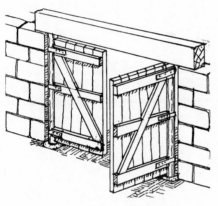

Figure 9-7A
Wood fortress gate

The Roman Campaign

Although Vespasian's legions were easily able to subdue those along the Judean countryside during the initial phases of the Revolt, the final blow against Jerusalem would have to wait, because the Emperor Nero died in 69 CE. Vespasian returned to Rome and was eventually himself declared emperor. During a two-year lull in military action, the Jews fought among themselves—the major groups were the priestly aristocracy, the middle-lower class, and the Zealots—and were unable to capitalize on Rome's temporary cessation of military activities.

In 70 CE, Vespasian's son, Titus, continued the punitive operation against the rebellious Jews. Along with the three legions Vespasian had brought—the Fifth, Tenth, and Fifteenth—Titus

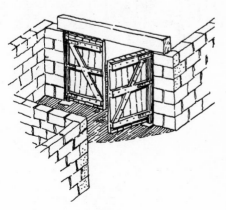

Figure 9-7B
Wood fortress gate at right angle to wall

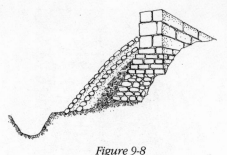

Figure 9-8
A glacis and moat

> *The camp, and all that is in it, is encompassed with a wall round about, and that sooner than one would imagine, and this by the multitude and the skill of the laborers; and, if occasion require, a trench is drawn round the whole, whose depth is four cubits, and its breadth equal. (Josephus, Wars Book III Chapter V)*

also had at his disposal the Twelfth Legion, which had been so unsuccessful in the early stages of the Revolt. The Tenth Legion set up their first base camp on Mount of Olives, overlooking the city of Jerusalem and the Temple Mount. Jewish commandos came out of their fortifications and attacked the Roman encampment. The legionnaires drove the Jews back behind the walls. Then Titus sent in reinforcements and counterattacked. He set up a series of base camps around the city walls and cleared the surrounding gardens and orchards to prevent the Jews from escaping, foraging, or staging any more surprise raids.

Titus then led an assault force around the north wall then toward the west. He assembled a file of archers between six columns of heavily armed infantry to resist any attacking force at long or short range.

In the meanwhile, his engineers began building earthworks *(Circumvallation)* and assembling battering rams, catapults, siege towers, and other war engines that they had transported cross-country. The earthworks with timber cribbing were to serve as platforms for positioning the catapults and siege engines. These also prevented the Jews from escaping or from replenishing their supplies.

Battering Rams

The largest battering rams built by the Romans were 100 feet long, operated by 200 soldiers, and could break down stone walls. The rams were made of metal-tipped wooden poles suspended by ropes from wood-framed towers on wheels. The soldiers rolled the towers up to the wall and covered them with wet ox hides to protect themselves against hostile arrows and flaming oil. See Figures 9-9 and 9-10.

Figure 9-9
A battering ram

Catapults and Pike-Hurlers

The Roman artillery consisted of catapults and pike-hurlers. Soldiers also could hurl javelins, missiles, and flaming spears *(falaricae)* a quarter mile in a flat trajectory. Figure 9-11 shows a catapult in action from loading to firing. Figure 9-12 shows three

But when they are to fight, they leave nothing without forecast, nor to be done offhand, but counsel is ever first taken before any work is begun, and what hath been there resolved upon is put in execution presently; for which reason they seldom commit any errors; and if they have been mistaken at any time, they easily correct those mistakes. They also esteem any errors they commit upon taking counsel beforehand, to be better than such rash success as is owing to fortune only; because such a fortuitous advantage tempts them to be inconsiderate, while consultation, though it may sometimes fail of success, hath this good in it, that it makes men more careful hereafter; but for the advantages that arise from chance, they are not owing to him that gains them; and as to what melancholy accidents happen unexpectedly, there is this comfort in them, that they had however taken the best consultations they could to prevent them.

7. Now they so manage their preparatory exercises of their weapons, that not the bodies of the soldiers only, but their souls, may also become stronger: they are moreover hardened for war by fear; for their laws inflict capital punishments, not only for soldiers running away from their ranks, but for slothfulness and inactivity, though it be but in a lesser degree; as are their generals more severe than their laws, for they prevent any imputation of cruelty towards those under condemnation, by the great rewards they bestow on the valiant soldiers; and the readiness of obeying their commanders is so great, that it is very ornamental in peace; but when they come to a battle, the whole army is but one body, so well coupled together are their ranks, so sudden are their turnings about, so sharp their hearing as to what orders are given them, so quick their sight of the ensigns, and so nimble are their hands when they set to work; whereby it comes to pass, that what they do is done quickly, and what they suffer they bear with the greatest patience. Nor can we find any examples whereby they have been conquered in battle, when they came to a close fight, either by the multitude of the enemies, or by their stratagems, or by the difficulties in the places they were in; no, nor by fortune neither, for their victories have been surer to them than fortune could have granted them. (Josephus, Wars Book III 214–218)

Figure 9-10
Siege of Jerusalem wall

catapults, a shield, and a *tortoise* (see section below on wooden shields) assaulting Jerusalem walls. Figures 9-13, 9-14, and 9-15 illustrate three different types of catapults.

They also used the Belly-Bow *(Gastraphete),* developed from the composite bow the Greeks borrowed from the *Scythians* (nomadic tribes from north of the Black Sea). It was an arrow-throwing weapon consisting of a composite bow horizontally mounted onto a wooden stock. A trigger attached to the stock held a cocked bow until fired.

Phillip II of Macedon, father of Alexander the Great, developed the catapult *(Katapultos),* using twisted sinew ropes. It consisted of a counterplate; a metal washer, which turned to impart tension in the sinew ropes; a hole carrier; and a supporting frame.

The *Trebuchet,* an improvement over the catapult, consisted of a gravity-driven engine that could throw a 300-pound missile 300 yards. It had only two moving parts: the beam and the sling. The beam was at least 50 feet long to develop enough leverage. A basket with weights hung from one end near a pivot. The other

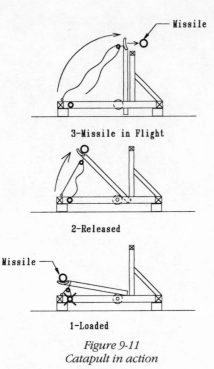

3-Missile in Flight

2-Released

1-Loaded

Figure 9-11
Catapult in action

As for what is within the camp, it is set apart for tents, but the outward circumference hath the resemblance of a wall, and is adorned with towers at equal distances, where between the towers stand the engines for throwing arrows and darts, and for slinging stones, and where they lay all other engines that can annoy the enemy, all ready for their several operations. (Josephus, Wars Book III Chapter V)

end held a sling for a missile or a basket loaded with heavy stones. With the anchor released, the beam rotated rapidly, flinging the missile in a trajectory toward the target. This war engine was sometimes used to throw a carcass of a horse across the fortress wall to spread disease among the defenders.

Ballista was a type of catapult that could throw a 650-pound stone 2,000 feet. A two-armed ballista was similar to a large mounted crossbow whose twisted sinew, or hair cord, was pulled back by a winch. Every legion was equipped with 55 ballistas, each with an eleven-man crew. *Scorpions* were similar but smaller than the ballistas and could hurl stones.

The *Roman Onager* had a single-armed hurling lever with a sling attached to its end. The gunners cocked the sling by a heavy, winch-operated cord. They mounted some onagers on a massive, wheeled platform.

Romans held catapult crews in high regard and separated them from the ordinary rank-and-file. They relied mainly on their well-trained troops but used catapults in sieges against fortified positions.

Figure 9-12
Catapults assaulting a Jerusalem wall

Assault Towers, or Siege Towers

During the siege, Roman engineers erected massive timber structures that they used against the city walls. They covered these assault towers with heavy wooden plank and ox hide for protection against arrows and flaming oil. Some towers had openings in the front for gangways or battering rams. Ramparts on top of the towers provided a protected platform for archers. See Figure 9-16.

Wooden Shields

Romans also used large, heavy wooden shields to protect their sappers while they removed the lower stone blocks from the walls. *Galleries,* or *Testudos,* also provided overhead protection. Galleries were movable armed shelters which attackers moved to stone walls in preparation for climbing or battering the wall. Testudos were shelters on wheels, with a heavy fireproof roof, to protect the soldiers during a siege. *Tortoises* were movable, heav-

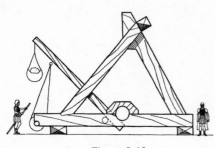

Figure 9-13
A catapult

ily protected sheds that were placed against fortress walls. Missiles dropped from the wall would glance harmlessly off the roof of the tortoise. The attackers used long wood ladders for climbing the walls.

The Final Assault

Roman engineers set up three battering rams northwest of Herod's palace and began their initial assault on the outer wall. They moved hide-covered wooden shields up to protect their battering rams. Then they built three assault towers next to the wall and positioned archers, bolt firers, and sling throwers on top. They fired down on the Jews who were on the ramparts and wall apertures.

Farther back, Roman artillerymen fired catapults in a devastating barrage. Jewish defenders within the city walls had to run for cover as they fled the rain of missiles hurtling down upon them.

The continuous pounding of the battering rams finally caused the outermost wall, the Third Wall, to give way. Legionaries plunged through the opening and forced the Jews to fall back to the Second Wall. Titus then called on his engineers to set up more battering rams at the southwest part of the city walls. It took five days to breach this wall; then, 1,500 legionaries rushed in through the opening into the marketplace.

Once inside, the attacking Romans found themselves in narrow, winding alleys more suitable for defense than attack. The Jews halted the Roman's advance in bloody hand-to-hand combat and forced them back through the break in the wall. The Jews then rushed to block the opening with stones and prepared for the next onslaught.

Five days later, Titus ordered his men through the wall again, and this time the Romans burned down the marketplace. There remained only a single wall separating the Romans from the Temple Mount.

Roman engineers worked under fire for 17 days to build another assault tower. In the meanwhile, two legions attacked the Upper City and two others assaulted the Antonia Fortress.

Titus planned to capture the Temple through the Antonia Fortress. He raised three banks of earth and rubble across the *fosse* and ravine, bringing in fill materials from sites 10 miles away. He planned then to burn the northern portico and attack the enclosure of the Temple.

Jewish fighters had accumulated about 150 catapults and

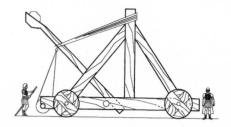

Figure 9-14
A catapult

Figure 9-15
A catapult

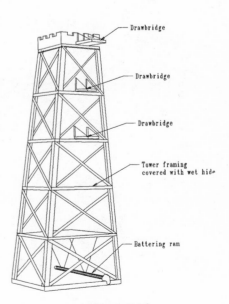

Figure 9-16
A siege or assault tower

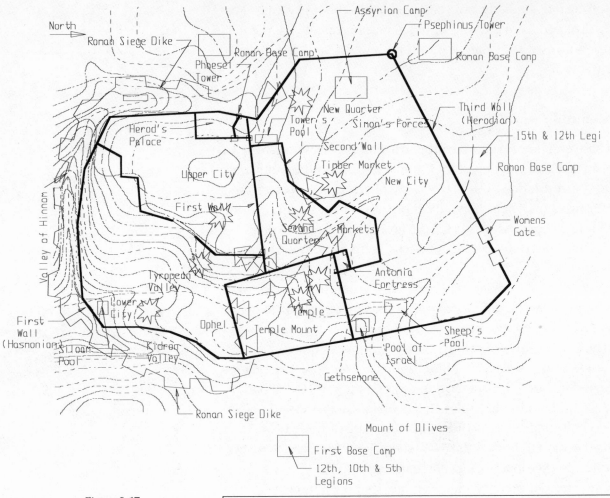

Figure 9-17
Siege of Jerusalem

> *Nor can their enemies easily surprise them with the suddenness of their incursions; for as soon as they have marched into an enemy's land, they do not begin to fight till they have walled their camp about; nor is the fence they raise rashly made, or uneven; nor do they all abide in it, nor do those that are in it take their places at random; but if it happens that the ground is uneven, it is first leveled: their camp is also four-square by measure, and carpenters are ready, in great numbers, with their tools, to erect their buildings for them. (Josephus, Wars Book III Chapter V)*

other war machines that they had captured four years earlier or had taken from Roman armories. They had also trained themselves to operate this equipment with effective results.

Jewish sappers dug tunnels under the wall against which the Romans were moving two assault towers. They shored the tunnel with wooden posts coated with pitch and filled it with combustible material. When the Romans moved their towers directly over the tunnel, the Jews set the shoring on fire. As the shoring burned, the roof of the tunnel collapsed, causing the two siege towers to topple over. Figure 9-17 shows the battle for Jerusalem.

The battle for Jerusalem became a succession of sudden attacks by the Jews against the siege engines and towers, only for them to be repulsed by Roman legionaries. Roman engineers had to scavenge greater distances to obtain new timbers to rebuild platforms and assault engines, which the Jews repeatedly destroyed.

This struggle continued for weeks until the Romans were able to position battering rams at the north wall of the Antonia Fortress. While the Romans were pounding the wall at one location, the Jews dug a tunnel under the wall in another, causing it to collapse. The Romans took advantage of the gap and broke into the city again.

Destruction of the Temple

After a month of bitter hand-to-hand combat, Roman soldiers finally reached the Temple Mount area and set fire to the gates. Metal hinges and locks melted from the intense heat, and flames spread to the roof framing and woodwork of the portico. The fire continued from one portico to another until all were ablaze.

Titus ordered his men to spare the Temple if the Jews did not use the Holy House in defense. But the Jews refused to surrender and continued fighting within the inner Temple courts. A Roman soldier, without waiting for orders, flung a blazing piece of wood through a window. The burning torch landed in one of the Temple's side chambers, and the flame spread to the wood paneling and roof framing until the entire Temple was on fire.

By the end of the day, most of the buildings on the Temple Mount were in flames. The Roman soldiers set fire to what remained of the porticos, gates, and treasury chambers. As the roof framing of the buildings burned, their unsupported stone walls collapsed.

When resistance by the Jews finally ended, Titus entered the city. He ordered the Roman troops to raze the city and the Temple, leaving only the *Phaesael, Hippicus,* and *Mariamme* towers and a stretch of wall enclosing the city from the west. The remaining walls encircling the city were leveled to the ground, except for the massive retaining walls of the Temple Mount. These walls were indestructible and still stand intact (War 7:1–4). According to Josephus, when the long battle had ended, the total number of casualties was 1.1 million (War 7:420), though Josephus has a tendency to exaggerate.

So ended one of the most significant battles in human history in which military engineers played a significant role. The War of the Jews lasted four years from the rout of the Twelfth Legion at Beit Horon to the destruction of the Temple. It took Titus only five months after setting up camp on the Mount of Olives to capture the Temple. The Second Temple was destroyed on the very anniversary, to the month and day, of the destruction of the First Temple by the Babylonians.

Chronology of the Siege of the Temple Mount

Key events leading up to and during the War of the Jews were as follows:

- Rome took control of Judea in 63 BCE.
- Archaleus was deposed and Judea was brought under direct Roman rule in 6 CE.
- Emperor Caligula attempted to have a bust of himself placed in the Temple in 40 CE.
- Gessius Florus looted the Temple treasury in 66 CE.
- Jews retaliated by destroying Roman garrison in Jerusalem.
- Zealots captured Masada and killed the Roman guards.
- Governor of Syria marched the Twelfth Legion on Jerusalem, which was trapped in a narrow pass of Beit Horon 12½ miles north of the city. Their equipment was captured by the Jews.
- Vespasian began an assault against the Galilee with three legions in 67 CE.
- Nero died in 69 CE and Vespasian was made emperor.
- Vespasian's son, Titus, took over the campaign against the Jews with four Legions.
- Titus marched the Twelfth Legion from Caesarea, the Tenth from Jericho, and the Fifth from Emmaus in camp on Mount of Olives.
- Titus was halted at Givat Shaul and sent 600 horsemen to reconnoiter. They were almost trapped by the Jews, who burst out of the gate and cut them off.
- Titus set up his main camp outside of Herod's palace. He built protective entrenchments and erected tents on Mount of Olives.
- The Fifth Legion joined the main camp.
- Titus moved the Twelfth and Fifteenth Legions to Women's Gate at the North Wall on May 24, 70 CE.
- The Fifth, Twelfth, and Fifteenth Legions breached the west side of Third Wall and entered the New Quarter on May 25, 70 CE.

- The Romans erected a second camp inside the new area, called Assyrian camp.
- The Fifth and Fifteenth Legions breached the Second Wall at Timber Market and entered the Second Quarter.
- Romans built a siege dike around Second City, Upper City, and Temple Mount on June 3, 70 CE.
- The Fifth and Twelfth Legions attacked the Antonia Fortress in July 70 CE.
- Antonia Fortress was captured; Romans entered the Temple Esplanade in August 70 CE.
- The Temple was destroyed in September 70 CE.
- Romans entered the Lower City from the Temple area and through First Wall.
- Lower City was destroyed

Epilogue

Vespasian and Titus celebrated victory by parading captured leaders Simon bar Gioras and John of Gischala, along with religious objects of the Temple. Two triumphal arches were built in Rome, which were inscribed as follows:

> The senate and people of Rome [dedicate this arch] to Emperor Titus . . . because of the guidance and planning of his father. He subdued the Jewish people and destroyed the city of Jerusalem, which all generals, kings and peoples before him had either attacked without success or left entirely unassailed. (Encyclopedia Judaica, p. 1167)

The destruction of the Temple was not the end of the Jewish people. New institutions and ideologies were born. Synagogues replaced the Temple; rabbis and scholars replaced the priests and sacrificial cult. The Rabbinical Period had begun.

Until the Umayyad Period (683 CE), the Temple Mount remained in ruins. During this period, Abdul-Malek Ibn Marawan, the Caliph of Damascus, built the *Dome of the Chain* (Dome of the Rock). They also built the Aqsa Mosque at this time.

Abbasides repaired the structures in 831, but earthquakes damaged the buildings in 1016 and 1067. The Fatimites, who succeeded Abbasides, repaired the Dome. From 1099 to 1187, the Crusaders conquered and occupied Jerusalem. They converted the Dome into a sanctuary dedicated to St. James and called *Templum Domini.* In 1187 Saladin defeated the Crusaders and stripped the Dome of its Christian paintings and icons. From 1270 to 1470 the Manelukes restored and repaired the Dome. In 1448 they refinished the fire-damaged Dome with mosaic tiles.

The Ottoman Turks conquered Jerusalem in 1517 and controlled the Temple Mount for 400 years. Suleiman the Magnificent continued the repair on the Dome and built the upper stone walls that presently surround the Temple Mount. After the Western Allies defeated the Turks in World War I, the British gained control of the Temple Mount but established the Supreme Muslim Council to maintain control of its buildings.

In 1948, during the Arab–Israeli War, the Jews conquered Western Jerusalem, but the Temple Mount remained under the control of Jordan. At the end of the Six-Day War (1967), the Israelis captured the Temple Mount.

For nearly 2,000 years, though ravaged by nature, warfare, and rebuilding, the Temple Mount remains unchanged. That is why its story is so formidable and challenging.

A

Abacus: a slab at the top of a Doric column or its capital; a device used for calculating. 60

Absalom's tomb: a stone tomb of the Hasmonean Period located on the east side of the Temple Mount. 21, 22

Acanthus leaves: architectural ornaments used in capitals of Corinthian columns, representing foliage of the acanthus plant. 113

Acropolis: a citadel usually located at the highest part of a city. In Greek, *acro* means highest point and *polis* means city. 137

Adobe: natural, sun-dried clay with a binder of straw or other fibrous material. 2, 15, 18–20, 59, 78, 79, 99

Adze: an ax-type tool used in chipping the surface of wood. Its cutting edge is perpendicular to the axis of the handle. 23

Aelia Capitolina: a town built by the Romans to replace the destroyed city of Jerusalem. 137

A-frame: a structure consisting of two wooden poles connected at the top, used for lifting heavy objects. 30–33, 35, 37, 75

Agora: a public area or market place usually located in the middle of a city or harbor. xix, xxi, xxii, 92, 114

Alabaster: a very fine stone through which light can be seen. See metamorphic rock

Altar: a place of sacrifice, built of a mound of stones or made of acacia wood and overlaid with bronze. xx, xxiv, xxv, 114, 118, 120, 121

Amphitheater: an open central area on which people sit to view sports or other events. 49

Ant: See *Antiquities.*

Anta: a pilaster, usually at a corner, whose base and capital do not conform to the architectural style elsewhere in the building. 21, 111

Antiquities: a book written by Josephus. 1, 18, 37, 44, 63, 88, 97, 105, 117, 119

Antonia Fortress: a structure at the northwest corner of the Temple Mount, built by Herod. 102, 103, 104, 107, 108, 113, 127, 128, 133, 135, 137, 196

Aphiprostyle: a building with columnar porches at both ends without a peristyle. xx

Aqueduct: a raised masonry structure containing a channel for carrying water from a source at a higher elevation. 53

Aramaic: an ancient language spoken by the Hebrews. 1, 4

Arcade: a series of arches supported by piers and columns, or a covered passageway. xx

Arch: a structure composed of separate wedge-shaped stones or bricks arranged in a curved line, so as to retain their position by mutual pressure. xvii

Archer: one who uses the bow and arrow; also a bowman. 125, 126, 128, 130, 132, 133

Archimedes: a Greek philosopher, inventor of the Archimedes Screw. 55, 70

Archimedes, Principles of: rules of physics developed by Archimedes. 55, 70

Architrave: the main horizontal stone beam supported by the column capitals; the lowest part of an entablature. See Entablature

Aristubulus: an ancient Hebrew king. 6

Ashlar masonry: masonry constructed of carefully hewn rectangular blocks in regular courses. 74, 75, 77

Assault tower: a wooden structure used to provide access to the top of a fortress wall or to support a battering ram for breaking through the wall. 132, 133

Astragal: the collar or small molding at the top of a Greek or Roman column. See Corinthian Order

Augustus Caesar: a Roman emperor. 6

Awl: a pointed tool used for boring or for chopping wood. It has a wooden handle and bronze or iron blade. 22

Axle: a shaft on which a wheel rotates. 28, 30, 42–45, 47

Axletree: a beam, fastened to the body of a chariot or cart, on which are attached the wheels. See Axle

Azarah: a place in the inner court where people gathered for prayer during the offering of the incense. xxiii

B

Ballisti: a type of catapult. See Catapult

Balustrade: a row of small columns, or balusters, joined by a rail, as an enclosure for altars and terraces. Also called a *Soreg* in Hebrew. 122

Barclay's Gate: an ancient doorway in the west retaining wall of the Temple Mount. 93, 94, 99

Baroulcus: methods of lifting heavy weights.

Barrel vault: masonry, archlike structure. 112

Basilica: a long rectangular building with two rows of columns dividing it into a central nave and two aisles. 54, 102, 106

Batter: recessing or sloping of a wall in successive courses. 90, 91

Battering ram: an ancient engine of war used to beat down the walls of a besieged place, consisting of a large wooden beam with an iron head resembling the head of a ram. 35, 128–130, 132, 133, 135

Bedding joint: the horizontal joint in a masonry wall. 69, 74, 77, 78

Bellows: an instrument for producing a strong current of air, as for blowing a fire in a kiln or furnace. 2, 19, 20, 23

Bema: a platform used by orators. 98

Bitumen: a mixture of hydrocarbons and other substances found in asphalt or tar. 2, 107, 127, 134

Block: a pulley used with ropes and tackle, consisting of a slim oval shell of wood. Inside ropes run around one or more sheaves (pulley wheels). See Block and Tackle

Block and tackle: a set of pulleys, or blocks, and ropes used for lifting heavy objects. 28, 29, 33, 53

Bonding: arrangement or overlapping of stones or bricks to tie a wall together. 90

Boning rods: a set of three wooden rods used by stone cutters. Two rods are connected from the tops by a string and placed vertically on opposite sides of the unfinished stone surface. After the string is pulled taut, the third rod is slid vertically under or next to the string, which rises above it when part of the stone is higher than the rest. The stone is then chiseled down to a smooth plane. 141

Book: a roll of parchment or papyrus. Also called a volume. 62, 63

Boss: the raised central portion of a stone block. 86

Bow: a strip of flexible wood bent by a string attached to the ends and used for shooting arrows. 42, 64, 65, 126, 128, 131, 132

Bowshot: the range or distance an arrow can travel. See Bow

Bowstring: see *Bow.*

Brass: an alloy of copper and zinc. In biblical usage the word *brass* signifies copper or bronze. 19, 24

Breastplate: a piece of armor for the breast used by Roman soldiers. 19, 126, 127

Broken range masonry: masonry that is not laid in courses. 74

Bronze: a metal made from an alloy of copper and tin. 19, 20, 45, 71, 110, 115, 119, 126

Bronze Age: a historic period characterized by the use of bronze tools and weapons. 22

Bronze Sea: a large ceremonial vessel in front of Solomon's Temple. 120

Bulkhead: a wall or embankment built to retain or prevent sliding of land; an upright partition that divides the inside of a ship into compartments. 127

Bulwarks: Temporary ramparts of logs, a military construction designed for protection of attacking or defending forces. 130

Buttress: a structure built against or projecting from a wall or building for the purpose of giving it stability. 128

C

Caesar: the title used for the Roman emperors from Augustus to Hadrian, later applied to the heir presumptive. 6, 22, 25, 26

Caesar, Julius: Roman emperor. 6, 20

Caesarea: a harbor on the west coast of ancient Palestine. 25, 47, 49, 83, 136

Calcine: to heat at a high temperature, causing loss of moisture, but below the melting or fusing point. 79, 80

Capital: head or cornice of a column; molded or curved top of a column that supports the entablature. 23, 24, 26, 106, 110, 111, 118, 129, 131

Capstan: mechanism used for hoisting blocks or cargo, consisting of a vertical axle, drum, toothed wheel, and pawns fixed to the axle, which engage the toothed wheel to prevent the rope from running backward in the absence of pressure on the levers. 26–29, 31, 34–36, 51

Cartwright: a craftsman who builds carts. 42

Casemate wall: two parallel walls, a heavy outer wall and lighter inner wall, connected by cross walls, which form chambers, or casemates, between the two walls. As an added defense, these chambers were sometimes filled with stones. 128

Catapult: a siege engine for throwing pikes or stones. A large crossbow mounted on a pedestal. 25, 54, 56, 62, 124, 130–133

Cavetto: a type of cornice. 108

Cella: an enclosed central chamber or sanctuary of a Greek or Roman temple. Also called a *Nosa.* 120

Centering: a temporary wood shoring used for construction of stone arches and removed after the arch is completed. 111

Centurion: a Roman officer in charge of 100 soldiers. 127

Century: a hundred Roman troopers, or company. 124

Channeling (quarrying): cutting a groove into stone in preparation for splitting. 73

Cherub: an angelic being illustrated in ancient art with a woman's head on a winged lion's body. 113, 116

Choker (rigging): a short, close-fitting rope used to lift heavy objects. 2, 25–27

Chorobate: a wooden instrument used for topographic surveying. 24, 67

Circumvallation: a siege wall, or a stone dike. 130

Cistern: a man-made reservoir that is filled with rain water or water brought from springs. 13, 79, 98, 100

City-state: a society built around a city 2

Clepsydra: a water clock developed in 1600 BCE in Egypt. 2, 53

Clinker: a mass of incombustible matter fused together as in burning of coal. 79

Cloaca Maxima: an ancient drainage system in Rome. 100

Cloister: an arched way or covered walk running around the wall of certain religious buildings. 88, 97, 102, 105, 119

Coarse rubble: masonry work made of undressed stones of irregular size. 74

Code of Hammurabi: ancient laws of construction written by King Hammurabi of Babylon. 67, 68, 70

Coffers: recessed areas in a stone vault or dome that reduces the weight of the roof. See vault

Cohort: a military subdivision of a Roman legion. 124

Colonnade: a series of columns placed at regular intervals and used to support a roof structure. 109

Composite Order: a style of Greek or Roman architecture. 76, 110, 118

Corbel: a shelf or ledge formed by successive courses of masonry that stick out from the face of the wall. 109

Corbelling: an overlapping arrangement of stones, in which each course projects beyond the one below. 109

Corinthian Order: a style of Greek or Roman architecture decorated with acanthus leaves. 109

Cornice: the uppermost horizontal molded projection of an entablature, resting on a frieze. 109

Course (stone): a horizontal layer of stone. 109

Coursed masonry: masonry work laid in horizontal planes. 109

Courts: restricted areas in front of the Holy Temple, named Israelites', Priests', and Women's Court. xxi-xxiv, 3, 92, 104–106, 108, 114–117, 120–122, 135

Coverstone: a stone covering a tomb. 21, 98

Crane: a lifting apparatus for raising blocks or cargo. xviii, 22, 25, 30, 31, 54, 75, 77

Crassitudo: the shaft of the building column. 107

Crenel: one of the openings between the merlons of a siege wall or battlement. 105, 113

Crenelated wall: a fortress wall with openings through which defenders can shoot on those below. 105, 113

Crete: an island in the Aegean Sea southeast of the Greek mainland. 2

Crossbow: an ancient weapon formed by placing a bow transversely on a stock from which arrows are released. 132

Crown: the center keystone of an arch. xvii, 88, 111, 119

Cubit: a biblical unit of measurement, varying from 18 to 20 inches, or the length of the lower arm from the elbow to the tip of the middle finger. xix, xx, xxiii, 24, 64–66, 84, 86, 88, 90, 107, 108, 110, 115, 116, 118–122, 130

Cube root: a quantity of which a given number is the cube; as cube root of 64 is 4. 59

Cut stone (dimension stone): stone blocks with smoothly dressed beds and joints. 71, 74

Cyclopean masonry: rubble masonry made with very large, irregular rocks or blocks. 74

D

Dead Sea: a lake without an outlet in southern Palestine; also called the Lake of Asphalt and Sea of Salt. 8–10, 14, 16, 19

Debir: the Holy of Holies of the Jerusalem Temple. See Holy of the Holies

Dentils: a series of small rectangular blocks, protruding like teeth, as under a cornice. 109

Derrick: an apparatus used for hoisting and lowering weights, comprised of a boom secured at the foot of the mast, from which runs a block and tackle, controlling the elevation and traverse of the boom. 30

Dimension stone: see *Cut stone*. 71, 74

Dioptra: a type of Roman surveyor's transit used to establish horizontal planes. See Level

Dipteral: having a double row of columns. Used to describe temples. See Column

Dolerite: a very hard stone used for pounding through limestone. 71

Dolomite: a magnesia-rich sedimentary rock resembling limestone. 23, 27

Dome: a hemispherical roof constructed of shaped stones. xxii

Dome of the Rock: (also called Mosque of Omar) an Islamic structure built on the Temple Mount in 691 CE by Caliph Abd-el Malik; and was a Christian shrine (Templum Dominic) during Crusader times and was rededicated as a mosque by Saladin in 1186 CE. 137

Doric Order: a style of Greek or Roman architecture. 109

Double Gate: an ancient gateway having two doors in the southern retaining wall of the Temple Mount. 92, 93, 128

Dowel: a wooden or iron pin or tenon used to join two pieces of wood edgewise. 25, 69, 77, 110, 118

E

Eggs-and-darts: an architectural ornamentation carved into the entablature. 109, 110

Eleazar ben Simon: a Jewish leader during the Jewish War against the Romans. 123, 125

Engines of war: ancient artillery, machines used to hurl arrows, spears, and stones. Catapults and testudos. 25, 48, 54, 124, 126, 130, 132, 135

Entablature: stone superstructure carried by columns. 109, 110, 118

Entasis: swelling of the lower part of a column. 107, 109

Eratosthenes of Cyrene: a Greek astronomer and geographer known for his accurate measurement of the earth's circumference in c 276–195 BCE. 61, 63

Esplanade: a flat, open paved area used as a promenade. 84, 92–97, 97–99, 104, 118, 137

Essenes: a breakaway sect who lived and studied in Qumran for two centuries from the end of the Hasmonean Period to the time of the War of the Jews against Rome. 3, 5, 6

Etruscans: an ancient people who ruled Italy between the 8th and 1st centuries BCE. 53, 110

Euclid: an ancient mathematician. 5, 59, 70

Extrados: the exterior curve or surface of an arch or vault. 118

F

Falaricae: flaming spear launched by a catapult. 130

Falsework (or shoring) a temporary supporting structure. 134

Fathom: the space of both arms extended; a six-foot measure of length. 65, 86, 105

Feather (Quarrying): a device used for splitting rock in a quarry. 73

Fiber rope: ropes made from pine-tree bark, coconut hair, camel hair, horsehair, thongs cut from hide, cotton, jute, sisal, flax, or hemp. 2, 25–34, 39, 46, 130, 131

Finger: a unit of measurement, seven-tenth or nine-tenth inch. 64, 65

First Temple: Solomon's Temple. xix, 49, 76, 84–86, 114–116, 120, 136

Forge: a workshop in which metal is heated in a furnace and hammered into shapes for tools and weapons. 19, 20, 126

Fosse: a defensive trench or moat. 96, 104, 133

Frieze: central part of an entablature of a column that is between the architrave and the cornice. 22, 53

Frontius: Roman engineer (CE 40–103) who built aqueducts in Rome. 99

Fulcrum: the point of support by which a lever is sustained. 34

G

Galilee Sea: a fresh-water lake in northwest Palestine; also called Lake of Galilee or Kinneret. 6, 8–10, 13, 16, 83, 125, 136

Galley: a movable armored shelter which attackers moved to stone fortress walls in preparation for climbing or battering of walls. 49, 50, 51

Gangue: impurities in iron making. 18–20, 23

Gastraphete (Belly bow): a type of arrow-throwing catapult incorporating a horizontally mounted composite bow on a wooden stock. 131

Gate post: the post upon which a gate swings or one against which it closes. 71, 91, 128

Gentiles' Court: the outer court of the Temple Mount, permitted for public use. 122

Gihon Spring: ancient spring located near south wall of City of David. 13, 98, 101

Glacis: a sloping bank or defensive wall used against battering rams and to make approach more difficult. It is also effectively ricocheted stones dropped by the defenders. 103, 127, 129, 130

Gneiss: a metamorphic rock similar to granite. 13, 71

Gradient: degree of slope or inclination of an aqueduct or roadway. See Aqueduct

Greaves: shin guard, part of a Roman soldier's uniform. 126

Greek fire: a flammable mixture of naphtha, sulfur, and pitch used in warfare. 130

Gregorian Calendar: a revised calendar introduced by Pope Gregory XIII, with the help of Christopher Clavius (1587–1612).

Groin: intersection of two vaults. xvii, 112

Groined vault: a structure made by the intersection of two-barrel vaults. xvii, 112

Groma: a type of Roman surveyor's transit consisting of a pole and horizontal cross from which hang four weighted strings. When the strings hang parallel to the pole, the instrument is vertical. 24, 25

Gunwale: the upper edge of a ship's side where at one time guns were placed. 49

Guy line: a rope used to steady something being hoisted or lowered or to steady anything liable to shift in position. 30, 36

Gypsum: a mineral ($CaSO_4.2H_2O$) used to make plaster. 15, 71, 78, 79

H

Halyards: ropes used to hoist or lower sails, yards, or flags on a ship. 49

Hammurabi: a Babylonian king. 67, 68, 70

Hammurabi Code: see *Code of Hammurabi*. 67, 68, 70

Hand: a unit of measurement equal to 4 fingers. xxiv, xxv, 24, 26 64, 65, 108

Handbreadth: the width of a hand, or unit of linear measurement from 2 ½ to 4 inches, or a palm. 64, 65, 108

Handspike: a bar used as a lever for raising a weight by a capstan. 29

Hanuyot: see *Royal Portico*.

Hasmoneans: the family name of the priestly family popularly known as the Maccabeans. 3, 21, 86, 100, 102, 127, 128

Hastati: part of a Roman heavy infantry that is made up of the youngest men. 124

Hechal: the main hall or Sanctuary of the Holy Temple. 115, 116

Hel: a kind of platform surrounding the courts. xxiii

Hemp: a tough plant fiber from which rope is made. 26

Herod the Great: king of ancient Judea. xvii, xviii, xix, 3–6, 21–23

Herodian stone block: a unique block with a receding border and projecting face used on the Temple Mount. 74, 90

Heron, or Hero, of Alexandria: an ancient mathematician and writer. 70

Hezekiah's Tunnel: a tunnel dug by King Hezekiah to carry water from a spring to the inside the city walls. 13, 91–101

Holy of Holies: the inner chamber of the Sanctuary of the Holy Temple. xix, xv, xxiii, 115

Hoplite: a heavily armed foot soldier. 124

Hulda Gate: an ancient doorway in the Temple Mount retaining wall. 91, 92

I

Igneous rock: original rock, including granite, basalt, and diorite, that has solidified from molten state. 73

In antis: with a porch having two or more columns enclosed between projecting sidewalls of a windowless structure. xx, 115, 119

Intrados: the interior curve of an arch. xvii, 111

Ionic Order: a style of Greek or Roman architecture identified by a pair of scrolls in the capital; slender column with flutes. 21, 23, 24, 54, 76, 110, 111

Iron Age: a period in which use of iron superseded bronze. 19, 20

Israel's Court: an inner court at the east side of the Holy Temple, also called the Court of Man. 121

J

Jaffa: a port city on the west coast of Palestine. 47, 125

Judah: a region in ancient Palestine. 8, 16

Judean: of or pertaining to Judah. 4, 8, 9, 13, 49, 53, 61, 124, 125, 129

K

Kebesh: a ramp or gangplank. xxv

Keystone: the central wedge-shaped stone at the top of an arch that locks the parts together. xviii, 111

Kiln: a type of oven used to bake or dry clay or brick. 2, 18, 54, 81, 82

L

Lake of Asphalt: See *Dead Sea*.

Legion: Roman military force of 5,000 to 6,000 men and divided into cohorts. 102, 124, 130, 125

Legionaries: soldiers of the Roman legion. 102, 124, 126, 127, 132, 133, 135–137

Level: a surveying instrument used to determine a horizontal plane. 24, 25, 72, 86, 87

Lever: a bar used for lifting or prying. 22, 26, 34, 55

Lime: Calcium oxide (CaO), a white caustic solid made by calcining limestone and other calcium carbonate substances. It is used for mortar and cement. 16, 78–81, 101

Lime plaster: plaster made of dehydrated, crushed limestone. 79

Limestone: a rock consisting chiefly of calcium carbonate. 16, 23, 38, 48, 49, 71–73, 75, 80, 89, 100, 101, 118

Lintel: the beam over a door or window opening. 31, 34, 75, 88, 92, 94, 95, 109–111, 119, 128

M

Mahtah: a firepan to hold hot coals. xxiii

Mandrel: a bar to which an object is secured while being worked on. 34

Maniples: Roman battalion. 125

Mark Anthony: a Roman general. 6

Mason: one who hews stones into shape for construction. xxix, 1, 4, 21–23, 75, 76, 90, 92, 95, 96, 110

Maul: a kind of large hammer or mallet used especially for driving piles. 34, 35, 36, 73

Megalith: extremely large stone block. xviii, 1, 22, 25, 26, 28–30, 34, 38–41, 46, 71, 72, 75, 90, 93

Menorah: a seven-branched candelabrum. xxi, 115

Merlon: in a battlement, the solid part between two embrasures or crenels.

Metamorphic rock: sedimentary rock which has been remelted because of heat; includes gneiss, marble, quartzite, and slate. 73

Metope: rectangular panel between the triglyphs in the frieze of a Doric temple, either plain or with relief decoration. 112

Mid.: see *Midrash*.

Midrash: ancient Jewish commentaries on the Scriptures. xxix, xxi, xxiii

Minoan: of an early civilization named after King Minos from Crete. 2

Mishnah: a compilation of oral laws into a scroll, later known as the Palestinian Talmud. The first Halackhic Code after the Written Law. xxi, 1, 86, 108, 120, 121

Mishnah Middot: collection of Jewish oral laws written by Rabbi Judah the Prince about 200 CE. See Mishnah

Molten Sea: a ceremonial bronze vessel about fifteen feet in diameter that stood in the inner court of Solomon's Temple. 120

Mortar: a mixture of lime, sand, ash, and water, used for plastering cisterns and reservoirs to make them water-resistant. It is also used as a binder in masonry. 49, 74, 75, 78, 79, 81, 90

Mosaic: a type of artistic composition created by small pieces of various colored stones inlaid in a mortar of cement. 138

Mount of Olives: a hill on the east side of the Temple Mount. 130, 136

Mycenaean: of an early Greek civilization, named after Mycenae and existing about 1200 BCE. 2

N

Naos: see *Cella*.

Nation-state: a society built around a nation. 2

Nave: the middle part of a church, often including the clerestory. 102

Negev: a desert in southern Palestine. 8, 9

Nero: a Roman emperor. 7, 88, 124, 129, 136

Nicanor Gate: a gateway on the east side of the enclosure walls of the Holy Temple. 122

O

Obelisk: a tapering four-sided shaft of stone. x, 41, 42

Offset-inset wall: wall with salient and recesses to provide extensive areas of firepower to defenders on the wall. 106

Onager: an Asian wild ass; also type of catapult. 36, 132

Ophel: south hill of Jerusalem Temple Mount. 91, 127

Ox: a male bovine animal. xxi, 28, 29, 37–46, 48, 64, 75, 89, 90, 97, 130, 132

P

Parapet: a low wall along the edge of structure. 91, 119, 128

Papyrus: a paper made from the stems of the papyrus plant by the ancients. 5, 62, 63

Parchment roll: an ancient book or volume of writings. 62, 63

Parthenon: a monumental structure built on an acropolis in Greece. 77

Pediment: a triangular termination or gable of a pitched roof. 109, 110

Peristyle: an open courtyard surrounded by columns; a colonnade surrounding a building. xx, 115

Pier: a free-standing stone structure similar to a column but thicker and used to support an arch. 92

Pike-hurler: type of a Roman catapult. 130

Pilaster: a rectangular column that is part of a masonry wall. 21, 111

Pile: a tree trunk stripped of bark and pointed at one end that is driven into the ground and used to support a foundation or to serve as an anchor 28, 34–37.

Pile driver: a machine used to drive piles into the ground. 34

Pillar: a vertical stone structure used to support, or a column. 88, 105, 115, 119, 122

Pilumae: a javelin. 126

Pinnacle: the highest point of the Southern or Royal Portico of the Temple Mount. 92

Pitch: a viscous substance used for waterproofing. It is made from coal, tar, asphalt, or wood resin. 107, 127, 134

Pitch-faced stone: a type of finish to ashlar stone. 73

Plaster: mortar or cement used as a coating over masonry walls or as a binder between bricks or stones of a structure. 13, 15, 78–80, 100, 101

Plato: an ancient mathematician and writer. 70

Plaza: an open area in a town or city. 91, 92, 113

Podium: an elevated platform. 98

Pool of Bethesda: See *Sheep's Pool.* 99

Pool of Israel: a reservoir near the northwest corner of the Temple Mount. 99

Portico: a kind of porch fronted with columns, often at the entrance of a building. 102

Post and lintel: a type of structure involving two columns and a base (or lintel). See Lintel

Pozzolana: a volcanic ash or powdered rock mixed with mortar and used by the Romans to make hydraulic cement that hardens under water. 54, 78

Priest's Court: an inner court on the east side of the Holy Temple for use by priests only. 120

Principes: a military unit made up of seasoned Roman soldiers. 124

Ptolemaic Period: the era of the Greek philosopher Ptolemy or the Ptolemies, kings of ancient Egypt. 3, 4

Pulley: one of the simple machines for raising weights, consisting of a small wheel that moves around an axle and has a groove cut in its circumference, through which a rope runs. 22, 25–32, 34, 35, 55

Pythagoras: an ancient Greek mathematician who developed the Pythagorean Theory of geometry and trigonometry. 5, 59, 70

Q

Quarry: a place where stones are dug, cut, or blasted; a place where stones are squared. 71

Quarry-faced stone: stones whose faces are left untouched as they come form the quarry. 71, 74

Quenching: rapid cooling of steel in water or some other liquid, which greatly increases the strength but induces brittleness. 20

Qumran: an ancient settlement on northwestern shore of the Dead Sea populated by Essenes during the 1st century BCE. 3, 5, 6

R

Ram: a male sheep. xxi, 92

Rammed clay: highly compressed clay. 78

Ram's horn: see *Shofar.*

Rigger: one who works with ropes and pulleys. 25–27

Rigging: ropes and other equipment used for hoisting and bracing of poles. 25–27

Rip-rap masonry: a wall or foundation of stone thrown together without order. 74

Rise: the vertical height of an arch, between the spring line and the crown. 111

Robinson's Arch: an ancient gate in the western retaining wall of the Temple Mount. 93

Rocker: a wooden frame on which a block of stone was placed before being finished so that it could be more easily moved around. 25

Royal Portico: the southerly portico on the Temple Mount. 102, 106, 107, 113

Rubble masonry: a wall made of uncut stones, as they were collected. 74, 75

S

Sadducees: a small sect that flourished during the time of the Second Temple, closely 8ed with priestly families. 123

Samaria: an area in ancient Palestine. 9, 13

Samaritans: a small sect of people who claim descent from the Ten Lost Tribes, comparable to the Karaites. 21

Sanctuary: the main assembly room of the Temple. 84, 115, 116, 119, 120

Sand lime: a mixture of sand and lime used as mortar. See Lime

Sandstone: colored sedimentary rock composed chiefly of sandlike quartz. 54

Sanhedrin: supreme religious and judicial body of the Jews during the Temple Period. xxiii, 113

Sapper: a military engineer, who is trained in building and destroying fortifications. 127–129, 132, 134

Scaffold: a temporary elevated platform used in construction to hold workmen and materials. 26

Scorpion: type of Roman catapult. 54, 132

Scribe: a writer, teacher, interpreter, or copyist of Jewish Scripture or laws. 63, 70

Sea of Salt: see *Dead Sea.*

Second Temple: Herod's Temple or the restored version of Solomon's Temple. xviii, xxi, 1, 13, 26, 114, 122, 136

Shear legs: a derrick made of a pair of long timber poles placed as an inverted "V" with a rope and pulley at the apex. 30, 32

Sheep's Pool: reservoir upstream of Pool of Israel at the northwest corner of the Temple Mount. Also called *Pool of Bethesda.* 99

Shema: Hear! Word that begins the verse "Shema Yisrael" (Hear, O Israel). xxv

Shofar: a ram's horn finished as a simple wind instrument and blown to herald solemn occasions or the Jewish New Year. xxi, 92

Shohet: a ritual slaughterer.

Sicarii: fanatic religious terrorists who fought against Roman rule. 124

Siege: encampment of an army around a fortified place. 7, 48, 54, 101, 123–126, 136

Siege tower: see *Assault tower.* 132, 133

Siloam Pool: reservoir near southeast corner of City of Jerusalem. 13, 99–101

Skewback: a sloping surface that supports the end of an arch. 111, 112

Slake: to combine chemically with water or moist air. See Lime

Sling (rigging): a rope or chain by which loads are hoisted. 26, 29, 33, 131–133

Soreg: see *Balustrade*.

Spring line: the horizontal line at the base of an arch. xxvii

Stele: an inscribed upright stone monument or slab. 67

Stoa: a portico or hall with columns along the front. 102, 106

Stonecutter: a craftsman who cuts and shapes limestone, marble, and other soft stones, by drawing with a compass, straight-edge, and other drafting tools and shaping with cutting tools. 71

Straton's Tower: the southeast tower of the Antonia Fortress, used as an observation post over the Temple Mount. See Antonia Fortress

Stringline: a straight line made by pulling a string taut over two points. 76

Stylobate: a platform built of stone blocks, called orthostates, which supports columns. 108

T

Tabiah, House of: an area just north of the Salt Sea (Dead Sea) between Judeah and Nebala which Jonathan acquired during the Maccabean Period. 13

Talent: a weight equivalent to forty-seven or forty-eight pounds. 66

Tamid: daily burnt offering services. xxv

Tar: A distillation of wood or coal employed to waterproof wood, textiles, yards, or rope. See Pitch

Tectonic: referring to geology of the earth's structural deformation. 10

Tempering: moderate reheating of quenched steel (to temperatures below 727 C) to reduce brittleness caused by quenching. 19

Temple Mount: a man-made platform upon which King Solomon and King Herod constructed the Holy Temple and Porticos. 82, 84, 85

Tendon: a hard, tough cord or bundle of fibers. See Rigging

Terra cotta: material used for roof tiles and pipes, made from clay and baked in an oven like course pottery. 78

Testudos: shelters on wheels with heavy fireproof roof, used by ancient Romans to protect soldiers during siege operations. 132

Tetrastyle: a temple with four columns on the facade. xx, 115

Tiller: a bar fitted to the head of a rudder to turn the helm of a boat in steering. 49

Tin: a metal used, along with copper, to make bronze. 19

Titus: a Roman general and emperor. 70, 129–133, 135–137

Titus arch: Triumphal arch in Rome in commemoration of victory over the Jews. 137

Tortoise: type of a large wooden screen used as a protective screen for soldiers sieging a fortified wall. 131–133

Treadmill: a round mechanism operated by men to run a mill. 47

Triarii: a military unit of Roman soldiers consisting of the oldest men. 125

Triglyph: panels in the entablature. 109

Triple Gate: an ancient gate in the southern retaining wall of the Temple Mount, having three doors. 92, 93

Tufa: soft volcanic rock used by the Romans as building stones. 54

Tuyere: an opening in a furnace through which a blast of air enters which helps combustion. 20

Tyre: a port city in Lebanon. 50, 76

U

Ulam: the outer chamber of the Jewish Temple. 115, 119, 120

United Kingdom: the period from the last days of David, 973 BCE to 933 BCE, when the Israelite kingdom was divided. xviii

Unsquared stone: stone that is used as it comes from the quarry, without any preparation other than removal of very acute angles and excessive projections. 73

V

Vault: an arched structure, made of stone, forming a ceiling or roof. xvii, 80, 92, 95–98, 112

Vespassian: a Roman general and emperor. 123

Vitruvius (Marcus Vitruvius Pollio): Roman engineer, architect of the first century BCE, who wrote an important treatise on history of architecture, called *Ten Books of Vitruvius.* 6, 22, 25, 34, 44, 53, 54, 66, 70, 76, 79, 80, 100, 109

Volute: a spiral, scroll-like or twisted formation. A distinctive feature of the Ionic column. 111

Voussoirs: any of the pieces in the shape of a truncated wedge that form a stone arch or vault. 94

W

Warren's Arch: an ancient gate in the western retaining wall of the Temple Mount. 93, 94, 112, 127

Wedge (tool): a triangular metal or wood piece tapered for insertion into a narrow crevice and used to split stone or wood. 25, 26, 33, 55, 57, 72, 73, 94

Wilson's Gate: an ancient gate in the western retaining wall of the Temple Mount.

Winch: a small capstan turned by crank. 29

Windlass: a hoisting or hauling apparatus consisting of a horizontal drum on which is wound a rope, attached to the object to be raised or moved. See Capstan

Women's Court: an inner court for women, on the east side of the Holy Temple. xxiii, 47, 121, 136

Z

Zealot: a member of a group of Jews who wanted to get rid of Roman rule in their land. 6, 124, 125, 129, 136

Zechariah: Biblical prophet (c 520 BCE) who lived in Jerusalem after the Babylonian Exile and urged the rebuilding of the Temple. ix, 21, 22

Zenith: a vertical point of the heavens at any place. 61

BIBLIOGRAPHY

Academic American Encyclopedia. Grolier Electronic Publishing, Inc. 1990.

Allsopp, Bruce, *A General History of Architecture from the Earliest Civilizations to the Present Day.* London: Pittman, 1955.

The Amplified Bible. Grand Rapids, MI: Zondervan Bible Publishers.

Archer, Léonie J., Susan Fischler, & Maria Wyke, *Women in Ancient Societies.* London: Macmillan, 1994.

Armytage, W. H. G., *A Social History of Engineering.* London: Faber & Faber, 1961.

Avid, Nahman, *Discovering Jerusalem.* Jerusalem: Shikmona Publishing Co., 1980.

Aviezer, Nathan, *In the Beginning.* Hoboken, NJ: KTAV Publishing House, 1990.

Avi Yonah, M. *Encyclopedia of Archaeological Excavations in the Holy Land.* Jerusalem: Israel Exploration Society and Masada Press, 1976.

Babbitt, Harold E., & James J. Dolland, *Water Supply Engineering.* New York: McGraw-Hill Book Co., 1929.

Bailey, Albert Edward, *Daily Life in Bible Times.* New York: Charles Scribner's Sons, 1943.

Bateman, John H., *Introduction to Highway Engineering: A Textbook for Students of Civil Engineering.* London: John Wiley & Sons, 1939.

Ben-Dov, Meir, "Herod's Mighty Temple Mount," *Biblical Archaeology Review,* Nov./Dec. 1986.

Ben-Dov, Meir. Jerusalem, *Man and Stone*. Tel Aviv: Modan Publishing House, 1990.

Ben-Sasson, Haim Hillel, *A History of the Jewish People*. Cambridge, MA: Harvard University Press, 1976.

"Reconstructing Herod's Temple Mount in Jerusalem" *Biblical Archaeology Review*, XV, no. 6 (Nov./Dec. 1989).

"Herod's Temple Mount—Stone by Stone" *Biblical Archaeology Review*, XV, no. 6 (Nov./Dec. 1989).

Brown, Curtis Maitland, *Evidence and Procedures for Boundary Location*. New York: John Wiley & Sons. 1962.

Bruce, Fredrich F., *New Testament History*, Garden City, NY: Doubleday-Galilee, Doubleday & Co., 1971.

The Builders: Marvels of Engineering. Washington, DC: National Geographic Society, 1992.

Canaan, Gershon, *Rebuilding the Land of Israel*. New York: Architectural Book Publishing Co., 1954.

Carta's Historical Atlas of Israel: A Survey of The Past and Review of the Present. Jerusalem: Carta, 1977.

Carta's Historical Atlas of Jerusalem: Seafarers and Sea Fighters of the Mediterranean in Ancient Times. Jerusalem: Carta, 1976.

Casson, Lionel, *The Ancient Mariners*. New York: Macmillan Co., 1959.

Casson, Lionel, *Ships and Seamanship in the Ancient World*. Princeton, NJ: Princeton University Press, 1971.

Chellis, Robert D., *Pile Foundations*. New York: McGraw-Hill Book Co., 1961.

Cornfeld, Gaalyahu, *Archaeology of the Bible, Book by Book*. San Francisco: Harper & Row, 1976.

Cornfeld, Gaalyahu, *Josephus: The Jewish War*. Grand Rapids, MI: Zondervan Publishing House, 1982.

De Camp, L. Sprague, *The Ancient Engineers*. Garden City, NY: Doubleday & Co, 1963.

Derry, T. K., & Trevor I. Williams, *A Short History of Technology: From the Earliest Times to A.D. 1900*. New York: Oxford University Press, 1960.

Duncan-Jones, Richard, *The Economy of the Roman Empire: Quantitative Studies.* 2nd ed. Cambridge: Cambridge University Press, 1982.(1982).

Encyclopaedia Judaica. Jerusalem: Keter Publishing House, 1978.

Engineers' Illustrated Thesaurus. New York: Chemical Publishing Co., 1952.

Ferrill, Arther, *The Origins of War: From the Stone Age to Alexander the Great.* London: Thames & Hudson, 1985.

Fletcher, Banister, *A History of Architecture on the Comparative Method.* New York: Scribner's, 1948.

Geuthner, Paul, *Revue Belge d'art orientale et d'archeologie,* 1977.

Gilbert, Martin, *The Arab-Israeli Conflict: Its History in Maps,* 3rd ed. London: Weidenfeld & Nicolson, 1979.

Granger, F., *The Ten Books of Vitruvius.* Cambridge, MA: Harvard University Press,

Great People of the Bible and How They Lived. Pleasantville, NY: Reader's Digest Association, 1981.

Hamlin, A. D. F., *A Text-Book of the History of Architecture.* London: Longmans, Green & Co., 1904.

Hamlin, Talbot, *Architecture Through the Ages.* New York: G. P. Putnam's Sons, 1953.

Hodges, Henry, *Technology in the Ancient World.* New York: Alfred A. Knopf, 1970.

The Holy Bible, Authorized King James Version. Collins World.

The Holy Scriptures According to the Masoretic Text. Philadelphia: Jewish Publication Society of America, 1963.

The Holy Scriptures. Chicago: Menorah Press, 1960.

Isaacson, Ben, *Dictionary of the Jewish Religion.* Englewood Cliffs, NJ: SBS Publishing, 1979.

Jewish Encyclopedia (repr.). Hoboken, NJ: Ktav Publishing House, Inc., 1967.

Jones, A. H. M., *The Roman Economy,* ed. Peter Brunt. Oxford: Blackwell, 1974.

Keel, Othmar, *The Symbolism of the Biblical World: Ancient Near Eastern Iconography and the Book of Psalms* New York: Seabury Press, 1978.

Kemp, Peter, *The History of Ships.* London: Orbis Books, 1978.

Kenyon, Kathleen M., *Jerusalem: Excavating 3000 Years of History.* London: Thames & Hudson, 1967.

Kolatch, Alfred J., *The Jewish Book of Why.* Middle Village, NY: Jonathan David Publishers, 1981.

Kollek, Teddy, and Moshe Pearlman, *Jerusalem: Sacred City of Mankind.* Jerusalem: Steimetzky's Agency, 1972.

Kutcher, Arthur, *The New Jerusalem: Planning and Politics.* London: Thames & Hudson, 1973.

Landels, J. G., *Engineering in the Ancient World.* Los Angeles: University of California Press, 1978.

Laperrousaz, Ernest-Marie, "King Solomon's Wall Still Supports the Temple Mount," *Biblical Archaeology Review,* May/June 1987.

Living Webster Encyclopedia of the English Language. Chicago: Engish Language Institute of America, 1977.

Lockyer, Herbert, *All the Trades and Occupations of the Bible.* Grand Rapids, MI: Zondervan Publishing House, 1969.

MacAulay, David, *Pyramid.* Boston: Houghton Mifflin Co., 1975.

MacAulay, David *City: A Story of Roman Planning and Construction.* Boston: Houghton Mifflin Co., 1972.

Mansir, A. Richard, *A Modeler's Guide to Ancient and Medieval Ships.* Dana Point, CA: Monraker Publications, 1981.

Mazar, Benjamin, The *Mountain of the Lord.* Garden City, NY: Doubleday & Co., 1975.

Menen, Aubrey, *Cities in the Sand.* London: Thames & Hudson, 1972.

Merriman, Thaddeus, *American Civil Engineers' Handbook.* London: John Wiley & Sons, 1947.

Miller, John Anderson, *Atoms and Epochs.* Boston: Twayne Publishers, 1966.

Miller, Madeleine S., and J. Lane Miller, *Encyclopedia of Bible Life*. New York: Harper & Row, 1944.

Morgan, Morris Hicky, trans., *Vitruvius: The Ten Books on Architecture,* 1914. Prepared by Herbert Langford Warren. New York: Dover Publications, 1960.

Mubley, James D., "How Iron Technology Changed the World and Gave the Philistines a Military Edge," *Biblical Archaeology Review,* Nov./Dec. 1982.

Negev, Avraham, *Archaeological Encyclopedia of the Holy Land*. Englewood, NJ: SBS Publishing, 1980.

Netzer, Ehud, "Jewish Rebels Dig Strategic Tunnel System," *Biblical Archaeology Review,* July/Aug. 1988.

New Marked Reference Bible (King James Version). Grand Rapids, MI: Zondervan Bible Publishers, 1978.

O'Connor, Leo, "Building a Better Trebuchet," *Mechanical Engineering,* Jan. 1944.

Oleson, John Peter, *Greek and Roman Mechanical Water Lifting Devices: The History of a Technology*. Boston: Reidel, 1984.

Paul, Shalom M. and William G. Dever, *Biblical Archaeology*. Jerusalem: Keter Publishing House, 1973.

Quest for the Past. Pleasantville, NY: Readers Digest Association, 1984.

Ramsey, Charles George, and Harold Reeve Sleeper, *Architectural Graphic Standards,* 5th ed. New York: John Wiley & Sons, 1961.

Reader's Digest Atlas of the Bible. Pleasantville, NY: Readers Digest Association, 1981.

Reader's Digest Story of the Bible World, in Map, Word, and Picture. Pleasantville, NY: Readers Digest Association, 1962.

Reich, Hanns, and Moshe Tavor. *Jerusalem*. New York: Hill & Wang, 1989.

Reid, Richard, *The Book of Buildings: A Traveller's Guide*. New York: Van Nostrand Reinhold Co., 1984.

The Revell Bible Dictionary. New York: Wynwood Press, 1990.

Rossnagel, W. E., *Handbook of Rigging*. New York: McGraw-Hill Book Co., 1964.

Rowland, Ingrid, & Thomas Noble Howe. *Vitruvius: Ten Books of Architecture.* Cambridge: Cambridge University Press, 1999.

Sasek, Miroslav, *This Is Greece.* New York: Macmillan, 1966.

Schiffman, Lawrence H., *From Text to Tradition: A History of Second Temple and Rabbinic Judaism.* Hoboken, NJ: Ktav Publishing House, 1991.

Schiffman, Lawrence H., *Texts and Traditions: A Source Reader for the Study of Second Temple and Rabbinical Judaism.* Hoboken, NJ: Ktav Publishing House, 1998.

Schwartz, Max, *Machines, Buildings, Weaponry of Biblical Times.* Old Tappan, NJ: Fleming H. Revell Company, 1990.

Sed-Rajna, Gabrielle, *Ancient Jewish Art: East and West.* Secaucus, NJ: Chartwell Books, 1985.

Shanks, Hershel, "Excavating in the Shadow of the Temple Mount," *Biblical Archaeology Review,* Nov./Dec. 1986.

Shanks, Hershel, *Ancient Israel: From Abraham to the Roman Destruction of the Temple.* Biblical Archaeology Society, 1991.

Shanks, Hershel, "Ancient Israel," *Biblical Archaeology Review,* 1991.

Silberman, Neil Asher, *Digging for God and Country: Exploration, Archeology, and the Secret Struggle for the Holy Land, 1799–1917.* New York: Alfred A. Knopf, 1982.

Sitchin, Zecharia, *The 12th Planet.* New York: Avon Books, 1976.

Sitchin, Zecharia, *Genesis Revisited: Is Modern Science Catching Up with Ancient Knowledge?.* New York: Avon Books, 1990.

Smith, David Eugene, *History of Mathematics.* New York: Dover Publications, 1958.

Smith and Engleburg, *Egyptian Masonry*

Straub, Hans, *A History of Civil Engineering: An Outline from Ancient to Modern Times.* Trans. E. Rockwell. Cambridge, MA: M.I.T. Press, 1962.

Thubron, Colin, *Jerusalem.* Amsterdam: Time-Life International Books, 1976.

Volkman, Fritz, *"Temple Architecture:* What Can Archaeology Tell Us About Solomon's Temple?" *Biblical Archaeology Review,* July/August 1987.

Watson, G. R., *The Roman Soldier*. Ithaca, NY: Cornell University Press, 1969.

Webster's Encyclopedic Dictionary of the English Language. Chicago: English Language Institute, 1950.

Wheeler, Robert Eric Mortimer, *Splendors of the East: Temples, Tombs, Palaces and Fortresses of Asia*. New York: Spring Books, 1965.

Whiston, William, *The Works of Flavius Josephus: The Wars of the Jews*. Grand Rapids, MI: Baker Book House, 1979.

Whiston, William, *Josephus: Complete Works*. Grand Rapids, MI: Kregel Publications, 1981.

White, K. D., *Greek and Roman Technology*. Ithaca, NY: Cornell University Press, 1984.

Whitehouse, Ruth, & John Wilkens, *The Making of Civilization: History Discovered Through Archaeology*. London: Collins, 1986.

Wilson, Charles W., *Ordnance Survey of Jerusalem*, London: Lords Commissioners of Her Majesty's Treasury, 1886.

Winter, Frederick E., *Greek Fortifications*. Toronto: University of Toronto Press, 1971.

Yadin, Yigdal, *The Art of Warfare in Biblical Lands: In the Light of Archaeological Study*, vols. 2. New York: McGraw-Hill Book Co., 1963.

Yaggy, L. W., & T. L. Haines, *Museum of Antiquity: A Description of Ancient Life*. Chicago: Western Publishing House, 1885.

Zanger, Walter. *Jerusalem*. The Great Cities Library. Woodbridge, CT: Blackbirch Press, 1991.

DATE DUE

DEC 1 2 2012			
GAYLORD			PRINTED IN U.S.A.